Nick,

We hope you enjoy your copy of "World Class Pricing: The journey". Good luck with your pricing journey!

— Shveta
Marketing Manager

WORLD-CLASS
PRICING

THE JOURNEY

WORLD-CLASS
PRICING

THE JOURNEY

PAUL HUNT • JIM SAUNDERS

iUniverse, Inc.
Bloomington

WORLD CLASS PRICING: The Journey

iUniverse books may be ordered through booksellers or by contacting:

iUniverse
1663 Liberty Drive
Bloomington, IN 47403
www.iuniverse.com
1-800-Authors (1-800-288-4677)

ISBN: 978-1-4759-8037-0 (sc)
ISBN: 978-1-4759-8039-4 (hc)
ISBN: 978-1-4759-8038-7 (ebk)

Library of Congress Control Number: 2013904499

Printed in the United States of America

iUniverse rev. date: 04/16/2013

CONTENTS

Foreword

This book has been brewing for 25 years.

Paul began working in pricing consulting in 1988, while Jim, who was trained as an Industrial Engineer, was involved in helping turn around an aerospace company.

In 1988, the pricing discipline was just beginning to attract the attention of CEOs. In those early days, pricing projects primarily involved helping customers develop price lists, gain control of discounts, segment their market, and build more effective pricing structures.

Pricing research was in its infancy. Historical methods had not worked, and people were just starting to hear about conjoint analysis, a powerful new tool that we began to use, soon recognizing its advantages.

Pricing training was also a growing area for clients to enhance their institutional knowledge of pricing.

This was all very beneficial for clients, but there was one thing missing: an overarching philosophy for pricing. Paul was struck by a statement he had heard a pharmaceutical pricing consultant named Mick Kolassa make: "Pricing should be treated as a process, not an event." Intrinsically, Paul knew there were many different pathways to improving pricing, but he had not yet been able to coordinate them into a coherent, repeatable approach to achieving excellence—in other words, a process.

The turning point came when Paul shared his belief in pricing as a process with Jim. Jim's experience in the aerospace industry had given him a deep appreciation for the necessity of process excellence and a language for expressing it. He shared his vision of how process improvement should be attacked, and that was the beginning of what has become the Five Levels of World-Class Pricing Excellence, an approach to help companies systematically achieve pricing excellence.

We spent the next several years developing and refining the Five Levels of World-Class Pricing. To do this, we had to answer fundamental questions:

- What are the core processes of pricing?
- What are the sub-processes?
- What differentiates Levels 1,2,3,4, and 5?
- Does it vary by industry?
- What are the implications of a company executing different processes operating at different levels?
- How does a company benchmark where it is and lay out a plan for improvement?
- What payback can be expected as you move up each level?
- How long does it take to move from one level to the next?
- What are the infrastructure requirements that help a company consolidate at each level?

Now, many years after these foundational concepts were developed, the Five Levels of World-Class Pricing have been widely adopted. Many leading global companies have employed them as their framework for global pricing improvement. We also hear many pricing practitioners referring to the Five Levels, as they find it a valuable way of articulating their journey to the wider organization. Consequently, we have been asked many times, "when are you going to publish a book on the Five Levels?"

It took a while, but it is finally here.

This book is intended as a pricing primer on the Five Levels of World-Class Pricing. Each chapter deals with a different level of the journey, supported by examples of specific tools and processes characteristic of that stage. Case studies are provided to illustrate the challenges and eventual achievements of that stage of development.

We hope that you enjoy it and find it useful.

Acknowledgements

Many people helped us make this book a reality.

Sally Praskey has worked as a writer for us at Pricing Solutions over many years. She played a huge role in getting this book ready for publication, and we could not have done it without her. Thank you, Sally.

Greg Thomas, who is a partner at Pricing Solutions, has played such an important part in the company. Thank you for the wisdom and thoughtfulness you have brought to the manuscript and to all of your contributions as a partner.

A big thank you to Mary Cullen, who took on the role of project manager at a stage in the process when we dearly needed someone to shepherd this through to completion. Your enthusiasm, input, and commitment to seeing this book launched is much appreciated.

There are many other people who have made significant contributions to this book. In particular, we thank Emily McLean for her support in coordinating the charts and diagrams. And our thanks to Boris Matas for designing the book cover and helping us redesign the Five Levels chart.

Paul thanks his father and brother for their many contributions to his life, both professionally and personally. They are not only his family members, but also his best friends. And Paul would like to acknowledge his daughter Julia, who is kind and generous and fun to be with. What a great combination!

Jim would like to thank our many clients over the years who have challenged us to continue to fine tune our Intellectual Property. Jim would also like to thank Gina for her unwavering love and support.

We also express our appreciation to the Pricing Solutions consultants with whom we have had the pleasure of working. Your commitment and dedication to excellence have made a difference to our clients, and are inspiring to us.

And finally, we thank the clients whom we have had the privilege to serve over the years. Thank you for placing your trust in us and for allowing us to share the pricing journey with you!

PRICING
solutions

Overview of the 5 Levels

LET'S GET PERSONAL ABOUT PRICING.

This book is about how *you* can achieve pricing excellence, along with your company. It is designed as a pricing handbook, to help you accomplish this in a systematic way.

While there are many different routes to improving pricing, this book organizes them into an easy-to-follow roadmap, or *process*: **The Five Levels of World-Class Pricing Excellence**.

But before we start the journey, it is important to understand why pricing matters so much. In 1992, an article in the *Harvard Business Review* titled "Managing Price, Gaining Profit"[1] argued that pricing is the most important driver of company profitability (see chart below).

Pricing is the highest-leverage item a company has for impacting profitability.

The following chart demonstrates the impact of a 1% increase in price and no change in volume. The result is a 1% increase in revenue, which flows directly to the bottom line and increases profits by 12.5%.

	Baseline	1% Sub Optimization
Revenue	100%	101%
Costs (Fixed & Variable)	92%	92%
Profits	8%*	9%

Impact — (9%-8%) / 8% = 12.5%

*Long-term average profitability for S&P 500 companies.

This relationship has been shown many times in numerous publications and conference presentations, and it is an excellent message you can use to gain senior management support for launching an initiative to improve your organization's pricing process. It gives you grounds to argue that if pricing is significantly more impactful than costs, your company should devote at least a healthy fraction of the time it spends on cost control to managing prices. The natural tendency is to focus on costs because they seem to be within the realm of what the company can control. Pricing, on the other hand, appears to be governed by the invisible hand of the market. In this book, we will argue that pricing can be managed in as disciplined and rigorous a manner as costs.

But there are some important points to consider in this relationship. First, it ignores both margins and elasticity (or volume implications). If it were really this easy, pricing managers would simply keep increasing prices and wait for the profits to follow.

Furthermore, the value of 1% is not constant over time. It varies depending on profitability. Profitability ratios erode during difficult economic times. The 8% average S&P 500 long-term average profitability drops to 4% or less during a recession. Therefore, the value of 1% of price improvement jumps from 12.5% to a whopping 25%! So pricing is even more important in tough economic times.

Pricing is a relatively new discipline. Not too long ago, if someone had told you he was a pricing manager, it really meant that he was an "estimator." Usually, the person worked in the accounting department and managed the standard cost system. He had tricky decisions to make regarding the number of units over which to amortize development expenses, or whether to include overheads from a far-away factory, but for the most part, his role was pretty straightforward. Typically, these fledgling pricing managers did not command a seat at the boardroom table, but instead were the bane of the salespeople's existence. Their work was more administrative than strategic. Equipped with an early-generation spreadsheet or a mainframe system, their ability to manage a vast number of SKUs across a large customer base was limited. Consequently, inconsistencies in legacy prices were common. Ask why a company priced product "A" 15% above product "B" in the early days of pricing, and the answer was typically: "Because that is what we have always done."

Unfortunately, this relatively stagnant corporate gene pool made managing changes rather difficult. Take "Ray," for example, who embodied this early pricing manager for us. With 30-plus years at the company and only two more until retirement, he was not about to sign up to a major process change.

Finding executive sponsors willing to take on the change management task is an important first step. But for those who have never been exposed to the potential benefits of improved pricing, it is often not an easy assignment.

The last part of the argument that we need to tackle before we can expect you to embark on this journey is that pricing can actually be managed in a proactive way, and entails more than merely accepting whatever price the market offers. Pricing is a *process*. Everything your organization does is part of a process. No matter how *ad hoc*, disconnected, and unrepeatable it is, if people are doing it, it is a process.

We remember facilitating a group of executives at an aerospace company in the late 1980s. The v.p. of sales was having a difficult time with the idea that his work was a "process." Finally, the v.p. of operations stood up and said: "Everything in business is a process. If I take this pen and hand it to you, that is a process. I can be held accountable for giving you the pen. You can measure whether I gave it to you on time. That makes it a process." His point was clear, and 10 years later, as we worked out the initial concepts of World-Class Pricing, his speech was not forgotten. Pricing has a mission, an owner, deliverables, and measurements. As such, it can be streamlined, and the results tracked and systematically improved.

Our experience over the past 20 years in pricing has been that finding segments where your value is high or where your market execution has been poor can lead to margin improvements starting at 1% to 2%, and accumulating over several years of concerted effort to deliver 4% to 6%. Any journey worth taking seems daunting at first, but you have to take the first step to get started.

In the remainder of this introduction, we will lay the foundation for pricing improvement, and focus on the following core concepts: **The Five Levels**; **The Four Core Processes**; and **The Pricing Infrastructure**. In subsequent sections, we will delve more deeply into each of these concepts. Let's get started!

The Five Levels

In the manufacturing world, the recognition of production as a process is not a new concept. As re-engineering initiatives took hold in companies during the recession of the early 1990s, benchmarking soon became part of the exercise. The search for universal benchmarks led to the development of five levels of manufacturing excellence, and we began to draw the link to the World-Class Manufacturing framework.

As we discussed it, The Five Levels began to take shape. We saw examples of firms that were stumbling along. Others had strong internal controls that prevented anything happening outside of the norm. Still others were starting to spend time understanding their value proposition. Then there were the revenue managers in the airlines and hospitality industries who changed their prices constantly. Was this quest for, in one case, value, and in the other, revenue optimization a goal that was possible for all organizations to achieve? We came to learn that it was, and that maximizing profits without tackling the challenge of advancing pricing excellence was not possible. From this, The Five Levels were born.

The Five Levels of World-Class Pricing will help you benchmark where you are on the journey to Pricing Excellence, so you will know how to systematically move forward. It begins at Level 1 with the Firefighter, followed by the Policeman, the Partner, the Scientist, and finally, the Master.

Figure 0.1
Five Levels of World-Class Pricing

Each level is distinct, with its own issues. If you are a pricing manager, you will probably relate to the titles we have given each one.

Executing various processes at different levels is possible, but overall, a company will be operating at single level based on how it executes across all of the relevant pricing processes that exist—or do not.

Level 1: The Firefighter

At this level, the baseline process is ineffective. Pricing tends to be reactive and undisciplined. In other words, the company and the pricing manager are "firefighting."

Ray, whom we introduced earlier, was toiling as a Firefighter at Level 1. He worked in a medical-devices company that had leading technologies and market share in a number of categories. Ray was responsible for running the contracting process and making sure the appropriate prices were input in the contracts and then sent out to the sales team for review. When you walked into his office, it appeared to be well organized. Once you dug a little deeper, however, evidence of firefighting became obvious. For example, Ray was responsible for contract renewals. He would send out the more than 2,000 contracts to the sales team for review well in advance of the renewal date. Then there would be a back and forth with "price requests for deviations due to competitive conditions." Ray did not have the authority to make these decisions, so the organization created a pricing committee that included several members of senior management. The problem was that almost every deal was an exception, and senior management was spending an inordinate amount of time reviewing requested price deviations. This also resulted in a constant state of emergency in which Ray, the sales force, and the pricing committee were continually reacting to the newest priority. It was not pretty!

Level 2: The Policeman

At this level, a company gains control of its pricing processes, primarily by controlling discounting. The company starts bringing structure to its pricing, and begins to say "no" to deals, rather than constantly adjusting discounts. At Level 2, the company and the pricing manager behave like Policemen managing traffic. Rules are applied, and they are obeyed. They may not always make sense from the customers' perspective, but they do bring order.

We had one client in the financial-services industry who was a classic Level 2. Jeff was new in the job, and coming from manufacturing, he wanted to measure and control everything. He built spreadsheets of recent deals, total account volumes, and rebate programs. He knew what was going on because he could see it in his system. The sales team was unsettled by his insights, which often exposed unprofitable deals and led to the enforcement of rules; they found the system a barrier to "doing deals." Senior management, on the other hand, counted on his analysis, but admitted that it sometimes didn't take into account recent developments in a very volatile market. Jeff was the Policeman, but as such, knew a lot more about enforcement than strategy.

Level 3: The Partner

At this level, the company moves from an "inside-out" perspective to more of an "outside-in" customer-centered focus.

Level 3 processes are the Value processes. No longer is the pricing simply rules-based, but rather, it reflects the value of the company's product or service to the customer. At this level, the company and the pricing manager are creating a more collegial attitude towards pricing—one that everyone is more likely to agree to, since it is based on the customer's perception of value. For this reason, we call pricing managers at Level 3 the Partner.

Mike was the marketing director at a restaurant chain. Responsibility for pricing had just been dropped on his lap in the past 18 months, and we helped him gain control of pricing by putting in place tools and measurements for Level 2. Mike was a natural integrator of ideas. He had a good sense for the value of the brand, and had taken steps to keep a close eye on its evolution relative to an ever-changing consumer in the tough economic times of Q4 2008. He called one day to ask if we wanted to participate in his latest initiative—launching the Pricing Operations Council (POC), a group of a dozen store managers, area directors, and regional vice-presidents. It would be a chance for him to receive feedback from the field to ensure his pricing initiatives were on track.

Mike was forging a partnership with the field in which pricing/ value was the focal point for discussion. The charter of the Pricing Operations Council is shown below.

Pricing Operations Council Purpose

- To share with a select group of our operations partners the work we've been doing around pricing and how it's impacting the business.
- To gain the **benefit of your perspective and experience** as we continue to improve and enhance our pricing process.
  - A need for subgroups to help with key pricing initiatives.

- Develop a partnership between Marketing and Operations on pricing strategy, tactics, and decision-making.
- To work together to develop and implement Price Testing initiatives.
- To share in the success realized from good pricing strategy.

 Level 4: The Scientist

The movement to this level is often a subtler step, but its impact can be enormous. At this stage, there are two things taking place. First of all, the degree of precision around pricing sharpens, based on better customer data and insight being brought to the table. Choice-Based Conjoint analysis, pricing software, and multivariate regression models are all part of this equation.

There is also a cultural shift at Level 4. The company has created a culture of pricing excellence. The quality of discussions is different from those of companies that operate at Level 3. At Level 3, the discussions are very productive, but there is a gap in the data. At Level 4, this gap is filled. Improved data is available to the team, which leads to better questions, more robust discussion, and the ability to reach decisions more efficiently. Optimization can be a tricky topic in many industries. "We can't change prices every 30 minutes the way the airlines do" is an objection we often hear as pricing managers struggle to progress from simply managing value to optimizing pricing. We agree. Pricing optimization is defined differently in every industry. However, in each case it relies on measuring value, understanding how it changes by segment over time, and adjusting prices to respond to these changes and capture the economic rewards.

Guy was a salesman for 13 years before he took on the role of pricing leader for his company, which operated in the telecommunications market. Over the next five years, he moved his organization from Level 1 to Level 4. The key ingredients in his ascent were the implementation of value-based pricing and optimization tools, and the accomplishment of the arduous task of getting the sales force to buy in to value-based pricing. This was not an easy process, and took years of patiently implemented changes. But the results were dramatic, and Guy's company identified his division as best in class globally. He is now leading similar initiatives for other regions within the company.

 Level 5: The Master

The achievement of this level is rare, but that is the goal of any pricing manager committed to excellence. Once this level has been reached, the pricing manager has indeed become the Master. We have four simple criteria for accomplishing this feat:

- Intense commitment to value, and passion about pricing;
- Integrated business systems;
- Significant financial returns from pricing initiatives;
- Innovative approaches to addressing pricing challenges.

Greg was appointed as a senior-level pricing manager at a large consumer packaged goods company. Over the next five years, he transformed pricing at his company. He began by putting his team in place and then focusing on building credibility within the organization. His strategy consisted of two core prongs: change the culture, and drive process innovation.

Greg was the change agent for the culture; he conducted numerous training programs throughout the organization to strengthen the company's knowledge of pricing. At the same time, he hired a logistics expert to drive the process improvement while he took on the challenge of changing the management system and driving cultural change across the organization. As a team, they moved sales force compensation incentives from revenue to margin, put in place key performance indicators for measuring pricing improvement, and instituted cutting-edge tools for measuring value and optimizing price. After five years, the company was significantly outperforming the competition, and the president acknowledged to analysts that it had added more than $200 million to its bottom line through pricing excellence.

Similar examples exist in other industries, ranging from hospitality to software. There are many paths to Level 5, but they all have in common dedication to analytical excellence, cultural change, and an integrated business system.

Typically, we have seen it take 12 to 18 months to progress from one level to the next, so achieving Level 5 is a long-term commitment. But the rewards along the way make it worthwhile. There are generally 1 to 2 points of margin improvement for moving from levels 1 to 3, and .5 to 1 point for moving from levels 3 to 5. In businesses like telecom, where margins exceed 80%, the goal is often volume growth without price erosion. The opportunities Level 5 companies find to segment their market and increase revenue from creating innovative pricing structures are as significant as the margin improvement for a firm working with a 25% margin.

At what level do you think you and your organization are currently? If you feel as if you are operating at different levels in different parts of your business, you are not alone.

The Four Core Pricing Processes

While the Five Levels are intended to provide a benchmark of where you are today and some signposts along the way, you need to go deeper into the processes of pricing to create the roadmap you need to reach your destination.

Figure 0.2

Four Core Pricing Processes

These processes are universal. We see them in industries as diverse as heavy-equipment manufacturing, software development, food service, and financial services. No matter what you are selling, you must develop your strategy, decide how the strategy is to be applied to specific customer segments, execute transactions, and monitor performance.

In P1, you *develop a pricing strategy*. A solid strategy is the basis for achieving superior results. There is a saying, "I would rather have a poor strategy well executed than a good strategy poorly executed." We agree that execution is critical, but so is the strategy itself. Therefore, we would add another statement: "I would rather have an excellent strategy with good execution than a good strategy with excellent execution." An excellent strategy, if executed well, puts wind in your sails that will blow away a competitor who has merely a good strategy, even if it is executed with excellence. Strategy must be the first stage of the pricing process. To develop it retroactively based on summarizing recent transactions is like closing the barn door after the horse has gone.

Once the strategy is in place, the next task is to *set customer net prices*. This involves the application of pricing guidelines and rules that ensure fairness and enforce the strategy. Your company's route to market has a significant impact on the sub-processes of P2. If you sell direct to end users, for example, understanding customer segments and proactively slotting customers into these segments is key to P2. In a national B2C business, this might involve understanding local and regional strategies, such as pricing higher in the business district downtown than in a disadvantaged neighborhood. When selling through distribution, you have the added complication of channel compensation and often a shortage of information about end customers. P2 also involves the processes of determining which customers qualify for particular customer programs and investments. The concepts and objectives were established when developing strategy in P1. P2 is the planned execution.

The next core step, P3, is to *execute pricing*. At this stage, the company is executing the strategy with the customer. It requires that the front line be equipped with the tools that can communicate the value to the customer. P3 also incorporates the steps to ensure that the process can generate an accurate invoice. There should be procedures to maintain accurate pricing master data, and tools to ensure a smooth and efficient work flow.

P4, the final stage of the process, is *monitoring pricing performance*. Key performance indicators (KPIs) are developed and managed to ensure that the company stays on course and the strategy is sound. As a pricing manager aspiring to move up the Five Levels, KPIs can be a tremendous vehicle for helping you progress from Policeman to Partner. Policemen report the crimes at sales reviews; Partners coach the managers responsible to take ownership of their pricing results, and help them develop and implement plans to improve performance.

Many organizations lack the process orientation. Some telltale signs of process-focused companies: they have a corporate process improvement methodology; meetings run effectively; teams are organized around processes rather than functions (e.g., the order intake process would include all of the functional areas involved in that process, not just the order processing department); they know that they have high service levels, and why.

We often deal with service companies who find it difficult at first to see themselves fitting into the Five Levels and Four Core Processes.

Our experience with the service industry is that the emphasis might change, but the framework still applies. For example, financial-services companies go through each of the Four Core Processes, and can be benchmarked at one of the Five Levels.

One of our clients is a major bank that has several divisions, one of which provides loans to large multinationals. To create an effective pricing strategy, the division had to segment its customer base and build customized strategies for each segment. Then, when negotiating a deal, it had to set prices. Afterwards, it had to execute those prices, administer them, and finally, manage and measure them in the marketplace.

However, it is important to recognize the differences between services and products. The key distinction is that services are intangible, and therefore, defining the offering and communicating the value can often be a more difficult task. People cannot see or touch the service, so they must experience it before they can judge the value.

Let's now look at the how the Four Core Processes link into the Five Levels. If we use P4—manage performance—as an example, we can see how the overall competency of the company pricing process is determined. Policemen report results at Level 2. Partners, at Level 3, coach front-line managers in sales and marketing to address problems, and use what they learn about customers to improve their understanding of value. Scientists, at Level 4, have the trust of their colleagues to develop sophisticated pricing models that the organization uses to manage pricing more proactively. Masters—Level 5—are recognized for the value they have delivered in their evolution. We chose P4 here to illustrate the relationship of processes and pricing excellence or maturity, but P1 to P3 can be similarly characterized.

A company that can execute each of these processes at a high level of excellence is essentially operating at Level 5. However, organizations rarely execute all Four Core Processes in such a manner, and instead, have strengths and weaknesses in each of them.

For example, when it comes to setting pricing strategy, some firms have an innate understanding of what their brand means in the marketplace, but fail to consider how recent performance (P4) might impact their future strategy. Take, for instance, high-end fashion retailers in early 2009. Some brands (e.g., Coach) recognized that their consumers would be cutting back and would need to connect with the brand at a lower price point, while others held steadfast to their strategy as volumes plummeted. Effective pricing benchmarks and metrics (P4) can provide an early-warning system to help companies react more swiftly and with much greater precision to changes in the marketplace.

That's why, in order to get a true picture of how you are performing on each of the Four Core Processes, it is important to delve more deeply into the sub-processes. We have identified more than 40 sub-processes. However, some of these will vary across different industries. Below is a list of 17 that are relevant across *all* industries, which you can use as a benchmark to measure your own performance.

Figure 0.3

Four Core Pricing Processes

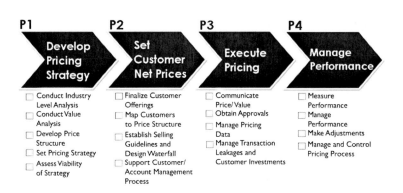

Companies may execute some of the sub-processes well, but others poorly. The key is to know which is which, and then build a plan to move forward.

Pricing Infrastructure

The final piece of the framework is the **Pricing Infrastructure**—the elements of the organization that support the pricing process. It consists of five areas: people, structure, objectives, system, and process.

Figure 0.4

Pricing Infrastructure

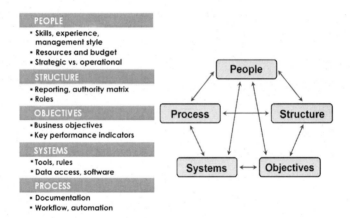

PEOPLE
- Skills, experience, management style
- Resources and budget
- Strategic vs. operational

STRUCTURE
- Reporting, authority matrix
- Roles

OBJECTIVES
- Business objectives
- Key performance indicators

SYSTEMS
- Tools, rules
- Data access, software

PROCESS
- Documentation
- Workflow, automation

Each element of the infrastructure is linked to the others, so a weakness in one part affects the whole.

Here is a brief introduction to the five elements of infrastructure.

People: The human element of pricing. How well do the skills of the pricing team match the skill requirements? Are there enough people to perform the required processing of transactions and analysis of opportunities and results? Do they have the network and credibility internally to advance the process?

Structure: The organizational structure. The reporting relationships that are in place are an important determinant of the pricing organization's ability to execute at different levels. For example, in the early stages of "gaining control" (Level 2), it is typical for pricing to report to Finance, but as the company drives towards value-based pricing (Level 3), it is important for pricing to report into Marketing. In Level 4, companies often have established a vice-president responsible for pricing. We have recently seen v.p. pricing, v.p revenue management, v.p. business analytics, etc. Sometimes, these functions include pricing as well as other operational excellence and strategy areas.

Objectives: Whether the organization has clear goals for pricing and the means for measuring whether they were attained. Most organizations have neither. For example, most companies execute price increases, but have no idea how much money from those increases was actually kept and how much was given back in further discounts or promotions to the customer. We also look at other reward systems. It's hard to imagine, but many organizations compensate the sales team on volume (in units, not even revenue!). Without a sales team that cares about margin, making improvements in pricing will be very difficult.

Systems: The tools, rules, data access, and software that the company has for ongoing pricing management. They can vary from very sophisticated software pricing optimization engines all the way down to simple spreadsheet models and legacy mainframes. Access to data is another matter. Some companies have excellent access, enabling them to make better decisions; for others, it is a highly manual process. It is important to understand the flexibility and limitations of the system before going too far down the path of changing the strategy and execution of pricing.

Process: The documentation of how pricing decisions are made and how pricing is managed. For example, a clearly stated pricing philosophy can help guide individuals, while a written process for pricing new products can ensure consistency and the application of best practices. Having a documented process means that the process can continue to operate effectively even if the pricing manager changes.

As you assess your organization, or plan to improve your pricing process, it is important that there is balance and cohesion across these five elements.

Let's start with Structure. There is no right or wrong way to organize your business for pricing excellence, but there can be a strong degree of fit or misfit between the elements. One of the most perplexing issues that companies must resolve is whether to centralize or decentralize pricing.

We recently met with the group sales team of a global hotel chain that was highly decentralized; its business was run from a number of corporately owned but highly autonomous hotel properties. The problem was that its pricing structure was contract-based and heavily negotiated, with each sales manager having a number of different levers to pull to win the deal. Furthermore, the corporate strategy was to hold the premium position in the marketplace. The chain offered more overall value than the competition, and wanted to be properly rewarded for the extra effort (and cost) that this model necessitated. Yet, there were no standardized processes for selling the value or delivering the service. Further, the system did not provide regional results much beyond a single P&L statement to each regional office, since the cost structure was not well understood. As a result, the objectives and results management were heavily volume-related. In that case, a salesperson would be foolish to spend time convincing an account of the value proposition when he or she could negotiate a price decrease and move on to the next account with little consequence. Therefore, the company chose to provide value measurement tools and training to the sales team, while aligning performance incentives. These tactics proved very successful.

Another company, faced with a similar challenge, centralized the pricing function, implemented systems improvements so the central team could keep its finger on the pulse of local pricing, and changed the incentive structure for the regional team. This strategy also worked very well.

In summary, there is no one answer for how to organize the pricing team, but changing one element of the **Pricing Infrastructure** must be considered in the context of the others.

Beware Broken Links

Remember that, as badly as you may want to improve the pricing process at your firm, pricing is linked to other core organizational processes. The pricing strategy must link with the overall corporate strategy (we believe it is a core part thereof). Setting Customer Net Prices in P2 must link with the account management process or the CRM process. Executing Pricing in P3 and compiling the information necessary to do so is part of the overall master data management process. Developing a price structure that your system cannot bill accurately and efficiently is of no value to your organization. Pricing KPI reviews are meaningless if they are not done in the context of the sales review process. Being a pricing manager requires that you are able to advance your agenda with the support of other key players in the organization. Building your team to include skilled change managers will serve you very well indeed.

By linking the **Pricing Infrastructure** to the **Four Core Processes**, an organization is taking a holistic look at pricing, and ensuring that improvements are made for the long term.

Summary

In this introductory chapter, we have developed the framework that we will use throughout the book. We have emphasized that pricing is a process just like other enterprise processes, and as such, it can be measured and improved. We have established the framework for the Five Levels of World-Class Pricing Excellence to mark your current position, set objectives, and plot a path forward. That progression involves process improvement, but there is more. The Pricing Infrastructure determines how robust your process is, and its ability to drive change. Ensuring a strong and dynamic fit among the five infrastructure forces will ultimately determine your ability to effect lasting change.

Implementing the changes will take time and patience. Progression from one level to the next typically takes at least 12 to 18 months. Why does it take so long? Pricing touches many different functional areas, and the changes in behavior that are required by each one will take time. There is a strong change-management component to pricing that must be considered. A good rule of thumb is that the people affected by any new process must experience it at least seven times before it is fully adopted and considered part of the ongoing process of the organization. We call this the "7x rule." If you prepare management to expect that the 7x rule applies to the changes you are implementing, you will have a much better chance of succeeding.

Level 1—
The Firefighter

Every business has a pricing process.

Sometimes, though, yours might seem more like pricing chaos than a pricing process. Many companies at Level 1 feel as if the sales force is in charge of pricing, which we liken to putting Dracula in charge of the blood bank.

We rarely find companies that are totally incompetent at pricing. Often, the problem at Level 1 is that pricing has been neglected, or it has been considered too sensitive or too big an issue to revamp. At the heart of a Level 1 pricing process may be well-intentioned managers trying to maintain order in the jungle. Sometimes, in an effort to bring a sense of control, they pull all decision-making close to their vest. But often in those situations, when you look a little deeper, you find that the inmates are running the asylum, as these managers thrive on the chaos. Consequently, Level 1 pricing managers are more likely to be type A personalities than sleepy-eyed bean counters. When you think of a firefighter, you naturally think of someone willing to risk his or her life in a dangerous environment for little reward. Pricing Firefighters in Level 1 companies usually fit this description well.

Pricing Firefighters frequently store a great deal of company pricing knowledge in their heads, and believe that this knowledge makes them invaluable and secure in their role. However, as you will see in subsequent chapters, a sharp analytical pricing manager can learn as much or more from the transactional history as the Level 1 manager has learned from his or her years of experience.

By the time we meet Level 1 companies, there has often been a changing of the guard. A new president or general manager has come on board and started to question the previous ways of doing things. Some of the old team may still be in place when we get there, but often the new manager has made a clean sweep. The lesson here is that simply trying not to rock the boat does not provide job security.

After doing a round of interviews through a Level 1 company, we met with the general manager. She was keen to know whether the years of experience that Mark brought to the pricing role were delivering value to the business. Unfortunately, we had seen no evidence of a standard process, no customer analysis, no in-depth understanding of customer needs, and no tools. Mark's team was manually inputting the same data in several different places in the system. "But what about his 25 years' experience?" the senior team asked. We struggled to find a polite way of saying that Mark actually had one year of experience 25 times over. Pricing, after all, is a journey, and without a vision for improvement and a desire to develop new tools and methods, you will be left behind.

In our experience, Level 1 pricing organizations fall victim to at least one of the following beliefs or situations.

1. **Cost-based pricing can work**. If cost-based pricing really worked, how is bankruptcy possible? In cost-based pricing, you simply take your costs, add the desired profit margin, and that becomes your price. Surely you would never add less than you need to be profitable. So

where's the problem? It's the fact that customers really don't care about your costs. They won't pay you more simply because your process is less efficient than that of your competitors. And it gets worse. As volume shrinks, there is a smaller sales base over which to spread fixed costs, so prices increase again. Customers leave and the death spiral continues. GM and Chrysler fell prey to this vicious cycle when they declared bankruptcy during the 2008 financial crisis.

2. **Cost improvements lead to lower margins**. Let's say variable costs for ABC Accounting are $800 to prepare a small business tax return. The company typically marks up 25% (to generate a 20% margin) and sells at $1,000. Through a new corporate training initiative, costs are reduced to $500. Using the same 25% mark up, the price is decreased to $625. Margin in this case drops from $200 to $125 per return. How could you justify a 100% mark up to keep selling at $1,000? We'll see in later chapters, but for now, let's stick with "customers really don't care about your costs." You might say this could never happen, but think about the case where there are thousands of items in the portfolio from hundreds of suppliers. Where is the strategy written down that tells the pricing analyst how to handle this when he or she comes across it deep in the pricing database late at night?

3. **They don't know their actual costs.** Many companies lack confidence in their costing information. Sometimes, they overestimate costs, which drives prices too high; other times, they underestimate costs, which leads to unprofitable pricing. Occasionally, the business is lucky; there are not that many offerings, and a strong general manager keeps prices moving in line with the market so costs are just one input to the price-setting process. But in one company, strict adherence to the strategy meant it left huge amounts of money on the table as it launched a new product. The company manufactured

heavy equipment—large trucks used in construction. It sold through distribution and, as is often the case with cost-based pricers, its distributors carefully guarded customer information. The company launched a significant upgrade to its existing truck, and thoroughly reviewed the costs before setting the price. Distributors jumped on the new offering, and soon the full order book meant long delays in fulfilling orders. The company also learned that distributors were taking more than twice their historical margins. The senior team convened to consider the problem. Surely there must be something wrong with their costing. They asked the accounting group to reassess the costs. A month later, Accounting reported that after reviewing every nut, bolt and piece of metal, the costs remained unchanged. So did the market price.

4. **Firefighters have a big red truck and are highly visible**. Not all Firefighters like to make a public display of putting out the blaze. Sometimes at Level 1, the pricing manager is more like the pointy-haired boss in the Dilbert comic strip, putting out fires and living the adventure in his mind rather than solving real problems for the organization. Take Patrick, for example. Patrick was the corporate pricing manager at another equipment manufacturer. He had worked to improve his skills as a pricer, and was clearly a very sharp fellow. He showed us a thick binder of analyses and models he had built. "Wow, have you shown these to senior management?" we asked. A long explanation ensued about corporate sponsorship, politics and a divided company, but the bottom line was that this pricing manager was stuck in his office. All the brilliant analysis in the world wasn't going to help a business in desperate need.

5. **It's not the best customers that get the best price; it's the best negotiators.** Level 1 companies have very poor controls and are therefore easy pickings for skilled negotiators. By instilling fear in the salesperson's heart

and understanding the weaknesses in the company's systems, good negotiators are able to swing deals that include free delivery, superior levels of customer service, and a host of other value-added features that make the deal unprofitable for the selling organization.

6. **Just because the business has been successful doesn't mean it isn't Level 1**. Sometimes a strong brand or powerful general manager drags a company beyond Level 1 through a conviction to be the premium price player. The problem is that if this manager moves on, the company will have no way of setting prices. See the case study that follows.

Case study: In Search of a Strategy Process

Matt was the pricing manager at a $1-billion manufacturing supply company. His business had held the price leadership position for much of the last 10 years. Whenever there was a "problem with the P&L," the company raised prices. The competition followed suit, and everyone made more money. But by late 2007, new offshore competitors weren't as complicit in making healthy margins on all product lines. They were more interested in buying market share.

Matt's company had a beautiful corporate office built from years of consistent performance. But this competitive condition was different. It seemed some products were still performing well, while the bottom had fallen out of the market for others. The senior team debated strategy, but had never been in this position before. A significant change in their market had rendered their existing process invalid. It had served them well, but was not robust enough to withstand change. We questioned whether what they had was a process or simply a strong-willed desire to be the price leader. But we believe the motto we developed in the Introduction needs to be refined somewhat as we progress. "A good strategy process will outperform a good strategy over the long haul." The strategy that had served this company so well for many years needed to be refined, but without a strategy process, they couldn't formulate the words: "our pricing strategy is out of date."

Four Core Pricing Processes

Assuming that your organization is not totally dysfunctional, why is it stuck at Level 1? Often, it's because there is a shortage of good information available. We have described pricing as a process, and in any process there must be feedback to help monitor and improve results. Therefore, we usually recommend starting with P4—**Manage Performance**. The benefit of starting here is that better performance information not only helps you be a better pricing manager, but it also starts to build your case for change.

Often, well-intentioned pricing managers are stuck at Level 1 because, despite managing their immediate span of control pretty well, they have never aggressively pursued the information they would need to capture the attention of the organization. Pricing is a powerful lever, and your first task is to show senior management the impact of current pricing decisions.

At one large and successful financial institution, we met Ron. He was managing a portfolio of products related to electronic banking for business customers. Ron was anxious to improve the pricing process in his area of the bank because:

- Discounting was excessive, and it seemed like none of the prices that the marketing department developed meant anything;
- Time to quote was increasing as the volume of special price requests was rising;
- It was 2007, and the quantity of electronic banking products was growing rapidly.

Clearly, Ron needed to resolve these challenges, or his department would be swamped in the massive shift to electronic banking that lay ahead.

So we asked Ron how he measured performance. He showed us a P&L statement that the corporate finance group had produced (too late and too infrequently), and told us he could never make any sense of the reports. Corporate allocations seemed random, and the numbers meaningless.

Ron presented us with the statement below. Upon review, it was evident that the corporate report was of little value in its current format. The main problem was a lack of any clear relationship between the volume and the costs at the variable level. This is where Ron had the most influence, but the presentation of the report provided little opportunity for him to analyze how that relationship was working.

Figure 1.1

P&L Statement Online Service Inc. ORGINAL VIEW

		Last Year				This Year		
			$0	%			$0	%
Revenue	Units:	4,791			Units:	5,071		
Net Sales			9906	100.0%			9,879	100.0%
Total Revenue (Price/Sales)		$	9,906	100.0%		$	9,879	100.0%
Implemenation Packages			145	1.5%			57	0.6%
Gross Profit			9,761	98.5%			9,822	99.4%
I/S Costs								
Data Processing and Communication			323	3.3%			379	3.8%
Data Storage Costs			253	2.6%			296	3.0%
Total I/S Costs			576	5.8%			675	6.8%
Net Profit			9,185	92.7%			9,147	92.6%
Support Costs								
Systems Support			497	5.0%			315	3.2%
Service Call Center			1,349	13.6%			1,702	17.2%
Sales and Marketing								
Marketing Expense			349	3.5%			439	4.4%
Sales Force			139	1.4%			214	2.2%
Management And Overheads								
Management			200	2.0%			600	6.1%
General Management			1,174	11.9%			494	5.0%
Allocated Costs			1,672	16.9%			816	8.3%
Total Other Expenses			*5,380*	*54.3%*			*4,580*	*46.4%*
Net Contribution to Overheads			3,805	38.4%			4,567	46.2%

Ron convinced us that motivating corporate to modify its reporting on his relatively small piece of business would be a monumental and likely fruitless process. But there was nothing stopping Ron from taking action on his own to generate the information he needed. The document he gave us had a great deal of information in it. Our first question was whether he could find out how many units his business had sold in the two periods. He had that data available, and it was inserted into the above chart.

We also started to discuss which costs were:

- Variable (changing with each unit sold);
- Product fixed (discretionary or incremental fixed costs that related directly to the product in question);
- Other fixed costs (the corporate allocations he complained about that came out of nowhere to impact the business).

And while it was true that we couldn't affect the overheads, the variable and product fixed costs were very important to the business, its growth and its pricing strategy.

When we re-organized the same information, we got what we call the "Pricing P&L," in which unit prices and costs are included and key costs are split into the three buckets above so that we can determine a margin.

Figure 1.2
P&L Statement Online Service Inc. REVISED VIEW

		Last Year				This Year		
		$ Per unit	$0	%		$ Per unit	$0	%
Revenue	Units:	4,791			Units:	5,071		
Sales at List Price		2,232	10,694	107.9%		2,256	11,439	115.8%
Discounts and Allowances		164	788	7.9%		308	1,560	15.8%
Net Sales		2,068	9,906	100.0%		1,948	9,879	100.0%
Total Revenue (Price/Sales%)	$	2,068 $	9,906	100.0%		1948 $	9,879	100.0%
Average Price (per month)		172.30				$ 162.36		
Variable Costs								
Imlementation Packages		30	145	1.5%		11	57	0.6%
Data Processing and Communication		67	323	3.3%		75	379	3.8%
Service Call Center		282	1,349	13.6%		336	1,702	17.2%
Data Storage Costs		53	253	2.6%		58	296	3.0%
Total Variable Costs		432	2,070	20.9%		480	2,434	24.6%
Marginal Contribution		1,636	7,836	79.1%		1,468	7,445	75.4%
Product Fixed Costs								
Product Management		42	200	2.0%		118	600	6.1%
Marketing Expense		73	349	3.5%		87	439	4.4%
Systems Support		104	497	5.0%		62	315	3.2%
Total Product Fixed Costs		218	1,046	10.6%		267	1,354	13.7%
Production Contribution		1,417	6,790	68.5%		1,201	6,091	61.7%
Overheads								
Sales Force		29	139	1.4%		42	214	2.2%
General Management		245	1,174	11.9%		97	494	5.0%
Allocated Costs		349	1,672	16.9%		161	816	8.3%
Total Overheads		623	2,985	30.1%		301	1,524	15.4%
Net Contribution to Overheads		794	3,805	38.4%		901	4,567	46.2%

We could see that, while list prices had increased, the realized price had actually *decreased*. We will discuss Variance Analysis in Level 2, but for now, see if you agree with our assertion that the volume gain did not make up for the net price decrease. The product fixed-costs story didn't look too healthy to us either. Marketing spending was up, and yet the business was not growing profitably. As well, systems support was reduced but call-center costs were rising. Was there a connection?

We went on to do customer research and develop a segment-based pricing structure for Ron's new product, but creating a P&L to help diagnose the problems was the first step.

The lesson is that better information is often within reach, and taking the time to report results in a way that helps you diagnose the problem is very important in setting the path forward.

Effective Strategy Can Compensate for Lack of Process—In the Short Term

In some cases, a highly experienced manager can mask a myriad of organizational weaknesses. This situation is common in smaller businesses where the founder/owner still runs the pricing process. His or her intimate knowledge of the value of the offer, customer needs, and how to align the two to capture value has led to a successful business. These managers make up for weaknesses in P2 and P4 of the process model with a strong (Level 3) understanding of value as they develop a strategy in P1 and the conviction to sell value in P3.

Figure 1.3
The Four Core Pricing Processes

Usually in these companies, processes are entrepreneurial or ad hoc. We will be talking a lot about models as we describe the **Journey to World-Class Pricing**. The pricing models in these businesses are mental models, meaning they reside in the brains of key individuals. But there are two problems with mental models: research has shown they have (somewhat) less predictive accuracy than subjective models, and much lower predictive accuracy than objective models; and they are not sustainable—eventually, the business grows to the point where the key individual can no longer be involved in every deal. How can a new pricing manager come into the role and be expected to assume responsibility for this mental model?

The average tenure in a management position in a Fortune 500 firm is about two years. Successful companies move managers around to keep people vibrant. There needs to be a clear pricing process in your organization into which a good manager can step and perform effectively.

Pricing Infrastructure

Unfortunately, the move out of Level 1 is more complex than simply establishing a control process or reformatting your reports. Usually in Level 1, there are structural problems with the pricing infrastructure.

Consider the following two cases.

Case study 1: Diagnosing the Problem

Some organizations thrive on the chaos of Level 1. Salespeople are put on pedestals (often of their own creation), and are beyond reproach. In one company driven to improve by an ambitious general manager, we met Curt. He was the regional sales director, and proudly told us that he was a "Hunter." He didn't have time for analysis or process. His role was to find new customers and sign them up. Curt was a horrific price-cutter who strutted around the office like a big game hunter. No one was willing to take him on, least of all a mere pricing analyst. In this company, the Firefighter in fact was the general manager. Pricing decisions were high-profile and dangerous. Only the GM was prepared to challenge Curt. Even the marketing director felt disconnected from the marketplace and unarmed to defend against Curt's threats of lost contracts. The pricing department was responsible for ensuring the contract

was entered accurately in the system. We were called in because the
GM was tired of his company's Level 1 pricing process.

If you were hired into a new role as pricing manager in this
organization, how would you start to address the problems?
Clearly, running the department as an analytical function
without a seat at the boardroom table would not take you to
higher levels of pricing excellence. Not every organization has
a "Curt," but there is so much at stake in a pricing decision that
you shouldn't assume that brilliant analysis will be enough to
carry the decision in the boardroom. We're early in the journey;
let's first make sure we diagnose the problem properly.

Returning to the infrastructure model, let's look at what is
happening here.

Figure 1.4

Pricing Infrastructure Model

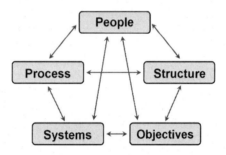

People: The pricing department today is staffed with clerks.
The primary protagonist is belligerent and self-centered. You
are going to need analytics to bring to your discussions with
Curt, but you should plan to spend time gaining his confidence
and designing a plan that helps him achieve his objectives while
you achieve yours. It would be too early to decide that he is
your mortal enemy.

Structure: Today, Curt and his team recommend the prices.
Marketing and Pricing start in a defensive stance. There has
been a process breakdown that accentuates the structural

weakness. Marketing has not been playing its role in P1—Set Pricing Strategy. With no strategy, Sales has stepped in to fill the void. Until the first iteration of a strategy and segmentation (P2) are in place, it is not a good move to wrestle for control of the pricing decisions.

Objectives: Today, neither Marketing nor Pricing has any skin in the profit game. Curt has been so possessive of pricing because he has felt that he has the most at stake. With few measures available, there is no way to know if anyone has been doing a good job. This may in fact be one of the starting points. Measuring performance and arming the general manager with some facts could begin to change the balance of power.

Systems: For now, systems are not a major hurdle. The current pricing team, with little else to worry about, has done a good job designing an efficient process of notifying the sales team of upcoming contract renewals and entering contracts accurately into the system. You should investigate whether the system is in fact capable of providing the type of data needed to support future pricing decisions.

Process: We have already identified the breakdowns in P1 (Strategy) and P2 (Segmentation and Customer Net Prices). There is a company planning process to which we can link the development of a pricing strategy. But we'll need to be somewhat patient here. Without much data to provide rich insight, the strategy for the first year is likely to be pretty bland. P4—Managing Execution—will yield data that can be used to counter the bluster and lead to better strategy development in the future.

Now let's look at a case study that has slightly different challenges in the infrastructure model.

Case study 2: People, Systems and Structure

Bob had recently been appointed president of a $400-million business unit of a major U.S. corporation. The unit had been organized to sell through 60 Local Market Centers (LMCs). The LMCs had profit-and-loss responsibility, and therefore the historical assumption was that their "skin in the game" was enough to ensure that local general managers were making effective price/volume/ profit tradeoffs.

But Bob's background was not typical for this company. He had come up through the data-driven world of a tier 1 Fast Moving Consumer Packaged Goods company (FMCPG). These companies trade on their brands (Coke, Procter and Gamble, Nestlé, Unilever, etc.), and their managers are trained to pour over market data to find segmented pricing opportunities to generate incremental profit.

When we explained that the range of management skills in these LMCs was between poor and good, he responded, "and this is what keeps me up at night." Using the infrastructure model to diagnose the problem, we identified a number of issues: a range of pricing capabilities and nothing in place to upgrade skills; a decentralized structure with control residing in the local markets; performance measures that were at such a high level that they provided little real insight (a simple P&L); no common processes; and no way to ensure that the people were using best practices to hone their pricing skills. This was a recipe for Level 1 pricing, and clearly, a lot of money was being left on the table.

Even worse, the lack of systems penalized some of the most diligent and conscientious analysts in the business. When I spoke with one such individual, Steve, he explained that corporate had "asked" for a 3% price increase for that calendar year. This business usually has 1,000 or so customers at each LMC, and often hundreds of SKUs at each account—in total, nearly 8,000 SKUs. Being smart and diligent, Steve developed a process. Without a unified approach to managing national accounts, he wouldn't be able to take price there. So he looked at the accounts that would need to be excluded because they were new acquisitions or had recently undergone a price increase.

That still left him a huge number of accounts, locations and SKUs. Unfortunately, prices were entered in the system as individual records rather than as a tier or percentage of list (which often didn't exist). Steve and his analyst spent New Year's Eve entering new pricing line by line, customer by customer into the "system," manually typing in new entries over old ones. We wondered whether accuracy had fallen off as the night wore on. Was there a process for measuring invoice accuracy? Typically not in Level 1.

Unfortunately, these companies often don't realize that there is anything wrong with their pricing process. In this case, poor systems were de-motivating the company's best people.

No one sets out to be at Level 1. Many may not even realize they are there. But as you can see, there are many dead-end trails. A small flaw in strategy, a sudden change in the market conditions, passivity towards a powerful IT department, a few strong characters in Sales can leave you bogged down in Level 1. We find it amazing how a few decisions can alter the course of a company's fortunes. But that's the leverage of pricing. The good news is that Level 1 is not a terminal (or even chronic) condition. We believe that Level 2 is within the grasp of every pricing manager who wants to get there. It takes the support of other functional managers, but not a fundamental redefinition of pricing roles and responsibilities. We'll save that for Levels 3 to 5!

Summary

Many of our clients embarking on the pricing journey ask if there is a Level-1. It is a humorous question, but it also reflects the loss of control they feel with their pricing.

The good news is that a major change is within their immediate and direct control, because the progression from Level 1 to Level 2 is not only possible, but also highly profitable. In fact, most companies will boost their profitability by between one to three points by making this journey.

However, do not expect the sales force to embrace this change. After all, that's like Dracula losing his coveted position at the blood bank. Now you will have to wean the sales force off price cutting and get them focused on selling value. That's the main challenge of this transition. Our experience is that about 60% of the sales team will make this transition seamlessly because they are already selling on value. The other 40% will struggle. Often, there is high turnover in the sales team at this stage unless the company provides solid training and adopts compensation practices that ease the change.

Level 2— The Policeman

The fires that raged in Level 1 have now been extinguished, and a new dawn promises to bring order to the pricing landscape. The journey from Level 1 to a solid Level 2 typically takes between six and 18 months to complete, depending on the degree of commitment and the access to good-quality data. We have seen it take longer, but that is usually an indication of problems with the systems that support the pricing infrastructure.

Where Do We Find Level 2 Firms?

Level 2 companies come in all forms and sizes, but it is more common to see a Level 2 firm in:

- Process-driven organizations;
- B2B rather than B2C;
    o companies that sell through distribution;
    o companies that have a high percentage of the business on contract;

- Companies that have recently implemented a system for improved data management and access (such as Enterprise Resource Planning or Customer Relationship Management).

We have seen companies launch Level 2 initiatives even before they have made a commitment to become better pricers. In these instances, the company is following a Six Sigma or other process improvement methodology, and someone raises the prospect of starting a pricing project under the process improvement umbrella. This approach will work well as the starting point if such a project involves understanding customer requirements, and defining and measuring defects. Companies using this methodology typically define a defect as a price that falls outside of the guidelines or that generates below-average margins, and they begin the journey towards measuring and controlling future pricing activities.

One caution, however: if this is your path into Level 2 pricing, make sure you define the scope of your project broadly enough to prevent people from pricing the products in your study high enough to conform to the guidelines, but then discounting elsewhere in the deal (possibly on other product lines or through a year-end rebate) so that no real improvement is realized.

B2B businesses are also a natural fit for achieving excellence at Level 2; typically, they sell through distributors or have a high percentage of the business on contract.

When selling through distribution, many companies fall into a trap: the distributors are reluctant to share information about the end-customer for fear they will be bypassed by the primary company. Consequently, information about the value of the offering is not shared, and so the company tries to treat all distributors the same, or runs promotions for which it has little information about the value delivered to the market.

Similarly, if a high percentage of the business is sold on contract, it is a major pricing effort to ensure that contracts are fair and profitable, and that customers are adhering to the terms.

Consumer packaged goods companies fall somewhere in between B2B and B2C categories. They think of their business as B2C, but they must sell through a retailer to the consumer. In order to manage the trade spending and promotions with the retail channel, these B2C companies must have strong Level 2 fundamentals in place.

The third instance of a robust Level 2 initiative occurs after a company has implemented a new ERP (Enterprise Resource Planning) or CRM (Customer Relationship Management) system. In these cases, there is a sudden abundance of information, well beyond what had previously been available to any single user.

Effective pricing management requires data from a variety of sources (transaction histories, contracts, account spending, costs, etc.), and the launch of a new system can drop a lot of information into the lap of the pricing manager. In some instances, the benefits of improved pricing were included as part of the business case for the system, but often, the new information creates a potential windfall opportunity for the pricing manager to exploit. The new system is a change to the pricing infrastructure that we introduced in earlier chapters, and we saw how important it is to rebalance the infrastructure once there has been a change in any one of the elements. In this case, it is an opportunity for the pricing team to develop new processes and measures using the wonderful integrated data from the system.

The Name Fits

We describe the pricing manager's role in Level 2 as that of a "Policeman" or traffic cop, a term that Level 2 pricing managers around the world have endorsed. In some cases, pricing managers have compared themselves to rodeo cowboys rounding up wild horses (while lamenting that it might be easier to herd cats), or exterminators shining a light in a dark room (causing bugs to scurry about in a frenetic dance). In most cases, however, "Policeman" aptly describes the pricing manager in Level 2.

It is true there is more to Level 2 than enforcement; the Level 2 pricing manager is deeply involved in creating the guidelines for pricing. But think of the Policeman as the cop walking the beat, setting the tone for how things will be done in that neighborhood. In our approach, we document the tools and processes, which is not typically a job that is required of a Policeman, but it will be important to your success just the same.

Case study: Chief of Police

Sam was a very good Level 2 Policeman. His company was already a process-driven organization. Stewardship was a responsibility it took seriously, and Sam was the global pricing manager responsible for shepherding the pricing process.

One of his first actions in his new job was to institute a pricing component within the monthly sales meeting. He established measures, and then worked with his regional pricing managers in three global regions to ensure that they had common definitions, that data was sourced in a similar way, and that they moved in lock-step to implement simultaneously at the regional sales meetings. He then worked to develop tools that could pull data from the organization's business warehouse and offer sophisticated reporting in MS Access and Excel.

Using the reporting tools, he acted more like the chief of police than the Policeman, as he spent his time ensuring that the regional pricing managers were taking action to prevent sales below guidelines, and that the guidelines themselves were reviewed as part of a regular process.

To ensure there was no question about how, when, and by whom he wanted the tools used, he got to work documenting his processes.

He was careful not to be too prescriptive when preparing the process documentation. He wanted to ensure regional ownership of the process, rather than having automatons that blindly obeyed the letter of the law and were not engaged in the business.

Finally, he implemented a global training program, first with the strategic and tactical pricing advisors who reported to the regional pricing managers, to ensure deep understanding of the tools and processes. He then offered more condensed classes for Sales and Marketing, to address and support the cultural change issues.

No Shame in Level 2

The downside of a structure with five levels is that senior management is not satisfied unless they are at the top rung. After all, this commitment to high achievement is what took them to the top. But we must point out that there is a difference between feeling satisfied and feeling secure. Pricing is a journey, and as your organization or career progresses, you shouldn't be satisfied with being a Level 2 pricer, as there is certainly room for growth. However, if you are a strong Level 2 with all the processes, tools and controls in place, you should be able to convince senior management that they can be secure in the knowledge that there is visibility and control, and that no one is going to "blow one by you." You might not be capturing all the money that is on the table—you need a good understanding of value before that can occur—but no one is robbing you blind.

Case study: Level 2 Leader

We were called in to do a diagnostic of a highly focused global consumer packaged goods company. Its products did not have mass-market appeal, but the consumers who bought them were highly loyal.

As we interviewed employees throughout the company, it became clear that the pricing process was operating in a tightly controlled band. Dates and milestones were mapped out, and everyone who was part of the process knew the name, sequence, and date of all the milestones. They knew what the deliverables were going to be at each point, and how they would use that information in their next phase of the process.

When running promotions, they looked at the return on investment, and compared that across the myriad of potential promotion opportunities.

They did a post-promotion review to assess how the event compared with expectations. They were concerned that the response to a promotion at one retailer might affect another, and had developed slightly different versions of their product to minimize direct comparisons. They had improved their cost-management systems to engineer cost out of their products, and their margin-management systems to make sure that cost reductions were not simply passed down the value chain.

Although they couldn't articulate exactly what created the value in their products, they did know they could command a premium in the market that they didn't need to give away as they re-designed their product and distribution systems. In our view, this organization was World Class at Level 2. The staff knew everything about process control, but only enough about value to know they shouldn't cut prices.

Senior management felt secure in the knowledge that the process was well managed, and indeed, company performance had been transformed since the new pricing process had been implemented three years previously.

Clearly, there was no shame in Level 2. This company had made tremendous improvements (6% margin improvement globally) by instituting this strong Level 2 approach. Still, the global pricing manager wasn't satisfied—he had a sense that he didn't know what he didn't know.

The company is now starting its journey to Levels 3 and 4 from a strong base.

Link to Other Processes

There are several lessons we can take from the "Level 2 Leader" case study and other Level 2 companies. One of the most important is that, while we call Level 2 "The Policeman," simply shooting the bad guys is not very effective policing. If you are the "Dirty Harry" (a take-no-prisoners cop portrayed by Clint Eastwood) pricing manager, sales will coin its own name for your job function: the "Sales Prevention Department."

One of the main attributes that distinguishes a strong Level 2 pricing manager from the "Sales Prevention Department" is the ability to link the pricing process to other core company processes. Later in the chapter, we will introduce the case of John, who was trying to implement pricing Key Performance Indicators. One of his many failures, however, was that he did not link pricing to other company business reviews.

By contrast, in the case study of the consumer packaged goods company, the pricing process was integrated with the business planning process. That ensured that pricing targets were established that were integrated and congruent with the financial plan for the business, and that cost reductions didn't result in offsetting price reductions. The pricing process linked to the key account management process, ensuring that key accounts were never embarrassed by other prices in the marketplace, and that the company was never caught paying a "make good" to support the margin of a retailer who maintained that the company's pricing process had put an unfair price into the hands of a competitor. The pricing process also tied into the product development process to ensure that new products and account-specific items were designed to hit effective price points at acceptable margins.

So as we look at the tools and processes of a strong Level 2 organization, remember that an effective cop walks his or her beat and is engaged in community policing (the process of building trust with members of the community to prevent crime), rather than just shooting bad guys. This stance will position you to gain the allies you will need to move to Level 3—The Partner—and will make Level 2 much more enjoyable.

Level 2 Processes

Level 2 pricing processes must touch all of our four core processes to some extent. In many cases, however, the pricing strategy is cost-based, which means the price structure is implemented fairly across the base of customers. This simple approach to P1 does not require in-depth analysis of the business and industry conditions, or deep understanding of the value that the company offerings deliver.

While there are some Level 2 pricing strategies that we will discuss later in the chapter, they form the launching pad for the move to Level 3. Consequently, we don't think of them as defining Level 2, even though they are part of it. Similarly, when it comes to P2 (Setting Customer Net Prices), Level 2 companies tend to do this more through strong control in the heat of the moment, as opposed to a proactive application of the strategy developed in P1.

That leaves P3 and P4 (Executing and Managing Pricing Performance). These two processes are truly the focus of Level 2 pricing organizations. If you think about Level 2 as being excellent in these two steps, it lends further credence to our comment that there is no shame in being a strong Level 2 pricer.

Figure 2.1

The Four Core Pricing Processes

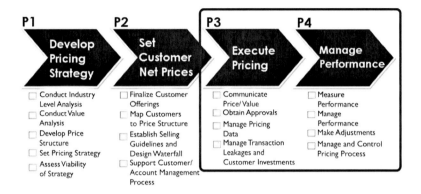

P3: Execute Pricing

Data Accuracy

To be effective at executing pricing, you will need to fulfill two primary criteria. First, you must put in place processes that ensure data is accurate, complete and accessible, and that the company authority matrix is up to date. Second, you must be in compliance with everyone who executes deals, being clear about the information they require and their responsibility, while ensuring that their decision criteria are well documented.

One of the biggest barriers we see to achieving these objectives is in the basic structure of the customer data. Remember "Mark" in the Level 1 chapter, who had a pricing structure that necessitated that the price of every product on contract had to be entered and managed separately? To make a change, his team had to touch every record in the database; the possibility of making an error was high. Level 2 companies faced with that situation will restructure contracts with customers to establish a discount percentage for a product group. Then if they take a price increase and the list price is changed, all contracts will be updated (even if there is an agreed lag or adjustment period).

Case study: Hitting Pricing Pay Dirt

When we met Stephanie, we asked her about the quality of her pricing data. She wasn't sure what she had; she'd never asked. So we immediately booked a meeting with her IT manager. "We implemented this new system about a year ago," he said, "and it captures every data element of every transaction. We were surprised that no one had ever asked what we had, but we have been waiting for the day to come when someone would want to use it." This was a dream come true for this business team. They had uncovered a gold mine of clean, accurate data. In this case, they had stumbled into it, but they could begin to analyze pricing in ways they had never before thought possible.

This led to the next evolution of the organization's development. It had been one of the firms described above that entered every customer price for every product. However, the IT person had been well prepared. He had established a structure whereby customers could be categorized according to the needs of the business team, and products could be discounted or rebated according to a matrix that aligned discount levels with different product groups. This process of product group pricing guidelines and customer categorization, as shown below, makes P3 much easier.

Table 2.1

Discount Structure

	Product Group 1	Product Group 2	Product Group 3
Customer Category A	8%	4%	3%
Customer Category B	9%	6%	6%
Customer Category C	10%	8%	9%

We are often asked whether a list price is really necessary. "The existing list prices are meaningless," the argument begins. "We have taken annual price increases on the list price, but have not been able to hold those increases in the marketplace, and so as time has passed, the list price has become less and less relevant."

However, we argue strongly for maintaining relevant list prices because they:

- Force product managers to stay in tune with the market;
- Provide a backbone to the pricing structure as described above;
- Make it clear what price to charge the one-off customer;
- Create a basis for measurement.

As we think about that basis for measurement, there is a case that stands out as the poster child for effective list prices. We were helping a company implement Level 2 processes, and were asking about different customer discount programs as we prepared to do a waterfall analysis (a waterfall analysis is a common Level 2 tool, and is described in more detail later in the chapter).

The general manager of the Italian business unit claimed that he had no discounts in his business and therefore didn't feel that doing a waterfall analysis was going to add much information. The next step in our project was a site visit, so we let it ride despite the challenges of the other GMs. When we arrived to review his data, we discovered he was correct: he did not have any other discounts in his price waterfall. However, his team gave huge price concessions that did not show up anywhere in the system because they hit above the revenue line on the division P&L statement.

A list price would have allowed the GM to capture these price concessions and compare them across business units. Furthermore, without a list price, other percentages on the P&L were being measured from a lower (net price) basis. As a result, proper diagnosis of other business issues was difficult. The GM argued that the factory was duping him on cost of goods because his percentage was higher than that of his peers. In reality, the percentage was being driven by a smaller denominator (net price) rather than a higher numerator (cost).

The other important reason for having an accurate list price is that an inflated list misdirects attention away from the importance of 1%. Consider the following example in which a 1% reduction in discount actually impacts pricing by 2.5%!

Table 2.2

	Base	1% More Discount	Change
List Price	100	100	None
Discount	60	61	1 point
Net Price	40	39	2.5%

This example has helped change the discounting culture at more than one company. Firms that used to argue about a one-point change in discount levels are now talking seriously about basis points (0.01%).

The next question, then, is: how do I set my net price? In this case, the answer is fairly straightforward. Ask Sales and Marketing: "what is the highest price you would expect to sell this product for to a customer who contacts you to make a one-off purchase?" You may be asked to analyze existing prices to see what the highest price is today, but at least now you have a price you can justify.

Managing the master data process requires diligent attention to detail. It is not a matter of looking for outliers or making performance comparisons. You can measure the number of invoice errors that need to be corrected in a period and slowly burn those down over time, but that is looking backward rather than being proactive. Doing an audit of the prices in the system compared to the physical contract document is laborious, but it truly puts you ahead of the curve in P3.

Authority Matrix

The other important step in P3 is managing the authority matrix, a company procedure document that outlines signing authority as different thresholds are reached.

Typically, salespeople don't like to have their deals scrutinized, and customers appreciate as short a sales cycle as possible. An effective authority matrix will fulfill that objective. In several instances, we have helped the pricing manager become a hero with the sales department by instituting a process whereby the system automatically approves deals when the guideline prices have been met. This shortens the sales cycle, motivates the sales team to sell for higher prices or lower discounts, and decreases the number of deals that management must approve.

In the section on pricing psychology, we will provide an example of price anchoring, to support the argument for having upper as well as lower guideline prices. We have certainly heard pricing managers complain that, when they had installed a pricing floor, the sales team had hit the floor and started to dig.

The next level of the authority matrix requiring regional sales management approval is that at which the annual business plan has been set. Prices at this level are set such that any deal below this level dilutes your ability to hit the business plan, and should be reviewed.

Prices at the next pre-set level are those that might prompt a competitor reaction, and therefore must be signed off higher up the management chain. While we don't advocate selling below variable costs, we recognize that there are relationship-driven businesses in which one product is sold as a loss leader to secure a broader relationship. In our opinion, these deals need to be signed off at the top of the business. After all, why do you want to be in a situation where the more you sell, the more you lose?

There are many different ways to establish the authority matrix, but the key points are to make it easy for good deals to move through the system, and to bring rigor and visibility to the deals that put your plan at risk.

P4: Manage Pricing Performance

There are three main levels at which pricing performance should be managed. At one level, you want to manage the performance of individual deals. How does the configuration of this deal fit into your overall pricing structure? At a higher level, you want to assess how your decisions have impacted the performance of the business. At a third level, you want to understand how much progress you are making with your pricing initiative (including both your financial progress and your journey through the 5 Levels).

We discussed data accuracy earlier in this chapter, and, while live reviews usually highlight any shortcomings in this area, the potentially negative impact on your credibility makes this a dangerous strategy. You need to have business leaders provide a sanity check of the data. However, if you do this in a public forum where your data is potentially showing their performance in an unfavorable light, their first objective will be to stop the pain, and the best way to do that is to cast doubt on your data.

Case study: Double-Check the Data

John had been working hard to implement pricing Key Performance Indicators (KPIs) over the past three months. He had spent countless hours with IT, pulling data and testing the algorithms to make sure that the Indicators were working just as he wanted.

The big introductory meeting was set. Everyone would be there. John had been satisfied with the enthusiastic responses from the area sales directors and product managers. They had all said they wanted to be more diligent in managing pricing, and that KPIs would be an important step.

The room was full, and John welcomed everyone to the first ever pricing KPI meeting. As he put the first Indicators on the screen, the room went silent. Then the questions started:

- *"What's a variance?" asked the v.p. sales. John was ready for this one, and gave a well-rehearsed answer.*
- *"I still don't get it," someone else chimed in. With another explanation, John was over the first hurdle.*
- *"I just reported my sales this morning at the Executive Market Review, and this number doesn't match," said a sales executive. Now John was stumped. "My guys get so frustrated with reports that don't match . . ."*
- *"Did you get these numbers from IS?" the controller asked. John nodded. "Then they don't include journal entries."*
- *"Well, my quantities don't match either," said another sales executive. John was flummoxed. Fortunately, the customer service manager was speaking: "When we process a return, we don't enter the quantity in the order entry system. That transaction is processed by the warehouse, so he is probably missing the return credits in his quantity calculations."*

- *"This seems like a lot of work,"* another executive was saying. *"See, I just look at this report I have always used. It gives me the sales numbers I need. I am not sure if this is adding anything."*

"Thanks, John." It was the president speaking. *"Jose, I wanted to talk to you about that new product initiative . . ."*

Question: Clearly, our friend John had a disaster on his hands. What could he have done differently?

Answer: John needed to make sure his numbers were accepted before the meeting. Setting up appointments with the people attending this meeting may have been difficult given their seniority, but at the very least he could have met with their key lieutenants, who could have vouched for the data accuracy and signed off on it.

A lack of data accuracy—or the perception of it—is a key stumbling block to a successful move to Level 2. Don't make the mistake John did!

Individual Deals

The development of indicators to track the performance of individual pricing deals has been well documented in other pricing books and articles. The starting point is the price waterfall analysis, in which all the costs attributed to a particular deal are tiered from the list price down to operating profit. Earlier in this chapter, we discussed the importance of having a list price. When you go to compare waterfalls from different deals, a list price offers a consistent starting point and basis for measurement.

In assessing your team's capability with waterfalls, you should be able to:

- Compare waterfalls easily across product lines, regions, customer segments, etc., through a simple tool that has drill-down capabilities. Linking the waterfall chart to an Excel Pivot table is the simplest way to do this.
- Ensure the accuracy of all variable costs, including distribution, trade or promotional spending, licensing, and cost of goods.
- Accurately allocate customer-specific costs, such as technical support, account management efforts, incremental costs for unique customer configurations, etc.
- Have an approach to the allocation of other fixed costs that is documented and agreed on by management. These include factory fixed overhead and depreciation, as well as marketing and head-office costs. Since these costs are simply spread like peanut butter across all transactions, this level of detail is the least important.

We use waterfall analysis in combination with the Price Dispersion chart. The Price (or Margin) Dispersion tool is another common Level 2 pricing tool. You need the waterfall in order to generate the data that you plot in the Price Dispersion analysis. The dispersion is simply the compilation and overview of all the waterfalls in a particular view of the business. So if you have developed drill-down capability for your waterfall, you will have it for the dispersion. As the waterfall fuels the dispersion, your analysis of the dispersion (identification of outliers) takes you back to the waterfall to help you diagnose and understand the underlying causes.

This cyclical approach is effective as you work with Sales to cultivate changes in behavior and, ultimately, increase profits. As we said earlier, being a good cop does not necessarily mean that all you do is arrest bad guys; a big part of Level 2 is teaching Sales and Marketing what these tools are showing you, so you can improve the business results.

One important application of these tools is using them to understand how individual deals, or groups of individual deals, fit into your price structure. We will talk later in this chapter about how advanced analysis of the Price Dispersion chart can help you learn about segments, and how the business strategy is playing out in the market.

Assessing Business Performance

Managing the price/volume tradeoff is at the heart of the business unit's purpose. Fundamentally, there are two steps required to make these important decisions: gathering and analyzing the appropriate data; and forecasting the predicted outcomes under different sets of assumptions. However, we typically find that businesses make pricing decisions based on gut feel and anecdotes because they have not completed either of these two steps with sufficient rigor.

In the end, the question lands on the desk of a senior manager who feels ill-equipped to make a sound decision. These executives worry about the impact of their decisions because they know they risk misdirecting internal resources, leaving money on the table or pricing their offerings out of the market.

As pricing managers, we strive to lead our organizations to implement best-in-class practices for decision-making and results management. It has been a daunting task to bring more discipline in managing the price/volume tradeoff, because accurate measures of price elasticity are elusive. However, that's where the Variance Tree can help define and analyze the appropriate data, and bring clarity to the price/volume tradeoff, even if we are not yet able to forecast the alternative outcomes with accuracy.

The Variance Tree

The Variance Tree aims to break business performance into its fundamental driving elements. It is similar to budget variance analysis in that we are performing comparisons (calculating variances), and splitting the performance metrics into sub-elements. However, the difference lies in two key areas: first, we are comparing actual to actual, rather than actual to budget; and second, we are focused on understanding what is driving the changes to the revenue line.

We compare current actual performance to a prior period because we want to see what has been happening to our business at the customer interface. The Variance Tree helps us understand how well we have performed, as opposed to highlighting whether we had high-quality plans and targets. Usually, comparing this year's results to the same period last year will provide the best insight, as it naturally removes any effects of seasonality.

Building a Variance Tree requires you to assess what is truly driving your business. The Variance Tree focuses on the revenue line (or customer margin line) of the P&L, and using price/volume/mix variance calculations, it decomposes changes in business performance to illuminate the business issues. For example, has the quantity variance (in dollars) decreased because we have fewer customers, or because our existing customers are buying fewer units?

Using a simple example of a chain of gasoline retailers, we illustrate typical factors in the Tree.

Figure 2.2

Variance Tree

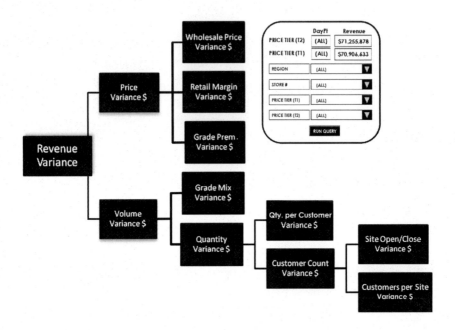

We make the first split between Price and Volume. The impact of price changes can be split further into changes caused by increases or decreases in the price of wholesale gasoline, the retail margin, and the premium we charged for mid and super grades of gasoline. Similarly, as we use the Variance Tree to understand the impact of volume changes, we can see a change in the mix of grades and the total number of liters sold. Working further down the Tree, the impact of quantity can be split into quantity per customer and number of customers.

Understanding the results in a quantitative way helps managers raise key questions about recent performance. The Variance Tree highlights how a promotion has (or has not) brought in new customers, impacted the mix, and affected average price per customer. The Tree should be built from the transaction level up, so managers can drill into item-level performance.

Case study: Decision-making with the Variance Tree

The Variance Tree has been developed as a key first step towards helping manage the price/volume tradeoff by decomposing the impact of recent decisions. This historical view can help challenge the mental models being used to make decisions. The same data can then be extended to translate historical performance into a forecast of future results.

In these challenging economic times, businesses are using price reductions and promotions to maintain volume. While the Variance Tree won't show what would have happened had you not reduced prices or offered the promotion, it will clearly show the impact.

At one chain of restaurants in the family dining segment, for example, managers chose to promote entrees at $5.99. This price point was considerably below historical average meal prices.

The result was a significant negative price variance (on the meals where the price was reduced) and negative mix variance from customers who traded down from higher-priced meals. And because the promotion was done as a stand-alone offer without a plan for bundling or up-selling, there was no offsetting increase in units per customer and nothing to offset the negative mix. Customer count variance was the only potential offset, and was the only unknown in the analysis. (How badly would customer count have declined if the promotion had not been executed?) The Variance Tree showed that, by not managing the risk of mix erosion, the business had to count heavily on the promotion bringing in substantial traffic. When that traffic didn't materialize, performance eroded. By thinking about the impact of decisions from the perspective of the Variance Tree, the business can articulate and quantify the risks it is taking.

Planning for Successful Implementation

As with any alteration to the business metrics, the development of a change management strategy is critical to a successful implementation. A framework like the one shown below helps teams think through the necessary organizational changes.

Implementing the Variance Tree is a change to the objectives setting and measurement process, and will require training to upgrade skills. One of our clients avoided the concept of mix for a year, until it turned from a positive to a negative variance. Then it became a key topic for managers in all functions.

The lesson is that timing and patience are vital in changing behavior. Process and systems changes will also be required. Where will the results be reviewed? How will they be linked to existing reporting? Finally, the ability to find reliable, accurate data that reconciles to other reporting will build credibility for your tool.

Figure 2.3

Pricing Infrastructure

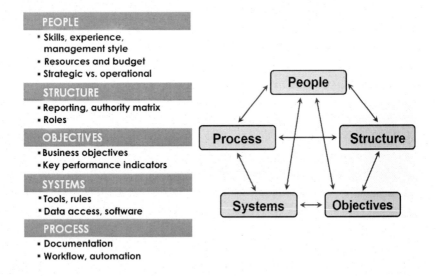

We have found that prototyping the tool using spreadsheets is a way to use real data as you build support for developing a more robust tool that integrates into existing review processes and performance objectives. It has also been effective for breaking accountability for performance into its composite parts. Going back to the example of the gasoline retailers, it is wise to make Marketing rather than Sales accountable for the mix of premium gasoline grades. Similarly, the regional managers have little influence on whether outlets are opened or closed in their area; that is the responsibility of Business Development.

As you build support for a Variance Tree, remember that designing the Tree is an exercise that is unique to your business and critical to the ultimate success of your initiative. Price, volume and mix are the starting points, but an understanding of the business is necessary to develop the next tier. We have found that experienced sales and marketing managers are a good source of input; this is where their gut instincts can be put to good use, and they are usually thankful to see metrics that help them sharpen their focus on the business.

A Continuous Cycle of Improvement

The Variance Tree is a step along the path to bringing greater certainty to pricing decisions. Ultimately, by having a projection of the volume impact under different pricing assumptions, you can forecast the profit impact. Adding the long-term impact on customer loyalty gives you a complete model. There are several steps to that goal.

Because the Variance Tree is built up from item-level transactional data, the variances can be broken into their composite parts. You can split the Mix branch into key items to see what mix tradeoffs customers have made and how these have affected the business. If results have been negative or unexpected, you can take action to remedy the situation. If customer counts have fallen in a particular region, and yet the rest of the Tree seems to be in line with overall results, perhaps a competitor has made a move in that area. If there are price changes in that region that are out of synch with the rest of the business, perhaps that regional manager has been too aggressive in taking price increases.

Once the problem (or a success) has been diagnosed, developing the solution becomes significantly easier; a problem well-defined is half-solved. Senior managers will naturally start addressing the accountability issues that this tool will uncover. They will also begin to rely on it to help them make future pricing decisions.

The Holy Grail on this journey is to develop an understanding of price elasticity—the percentage change in volume in response to a percentage change in price. It is difficult to determine price elasticity because not all volume changes are due to changes in price. However, with the data in the Variance Tree, you can begin to tabulate the history of price and volume changes. If you supplement this analysis with won/lost performance analysis, chronology of external events (e.g., promotions) or pricing research, it will sharpen the picture. And once you understand elasticity, you can build a forecast of volume and margin as a function of price. This is the point at which you have moved the business from managing on gut feel with mental models to controlling the price/volume trade-off with an objective model built on solid analytical principles.

Level 2 Pricing Strategies

Many companies at Level 2 have cost-based pricing strategies whereby they take the cost, establish a desired margin, and then calculate the price. That approach seems both straightforward and fair to customers. But if it was really that simple, how do you explain the prevalence of bankruptcy? There must be something, then, to the choice of the appropriate margin levels.

First of all, it seems intuitive that the more innovative and differentiated your product, the higher the margin you can seek. But this raises the next question: should all customers buying this offering pay the same price? We have a problem with two key variables: the expected margin level (price level); and how the margin should be shared with different groups (or segments) of customers (price structure).

The first challenge seems in some ways to be a bit simpler. The customer sets the price level. In the next chapter, we will discuss pricing for the value you create. But if your offer has been in the marketplace, it already has a price level. If not, please see the section on New Product Pricing in Level 3. For now, it seems obvious that the more value you deliver, the more you can charge for the product. Hopefully, costs are under control and higher prices lead to higher margins. However, in setting prices, compare the prices—not the margins—of the offers in your line-up.

Case study: When Price Trumps Margin

We conducted a study for a medical-devices company. It had many evolutions of its product, as it continued to leave older-technology products in the market after it introduced new, improved models. In several product lines, we found the newer "200" model priced below the older "100" model. We asked why the new, improved product was cheaper than the older version. After all, these were not computers, where technological obsolescence leads to faster and cheaper products each year. The answer in this case was that manufacturing had moved to Mexico. And while the company took a "slightly higher" margin on the new "200" model, the prices were still below those of the older version.

Remember that price can communicate value. In this case, where customers are buying a product that is medically but a better fit will improve comfort and hygiene, the pricing strategy was leading customers to believe the new product was somehow inferior to the older model. Even without knowing too much about the value of the products, we were able to improve the relative price levels by comparing prices rather than margins.

Pricing Along the Demand Curve

In a Level 2 pricing strategy, even if there is not a lot of information available regarding the value of the product, you can take advantage of a very powerful concept we call "Pricing along the demand curve."

Figure 2.4

Pricing Along the Demand Curve

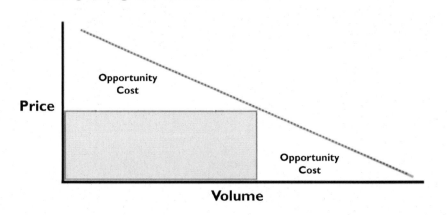

The downward sloping line represents the demand curve (although in this case with the axes flipped). There is more demand available at lower price points and less at higher price points. If we have only one product in the marketplace, notice that the revenue opportunity is represented by the single rectangle. But where is the opportunity cost? It is represented by the white triangle above of customers who would buy if you had a more expensive offering to sell them, and by the white triangle on the right of customers who found your offer too expensive and chose not to purchase. Clearly, if you provide additional, premium offerings for the segment above, and basic, unbundled offers to the customers on the right, there is a good chance to increase revenues and profits.

Two key points: first, this strategy requires effective segmentation and fences (see Level 3); and second, make sure that costs do not increase as you move to the right.

Case study: Publisher Prices for Profit

Several years ago, we were working with our client Carl in the publishing industry. His company sold advertising space to large national advertisers, important regional chain stores, and small mom-and-pop restaurants and retail outlets.

The national branded business was easy to manage. Carl's sales managers met with the nationals annually to work out "the plan," and then simply took the orders, printed the ads, and sent the bills.

Things were not so simple in the retail segment of the business. These customers were highly price-sensitive, as ad spending came out of their own pockets. But there were thousands of small accounts, and the publisher had set a goal for each member of the sales force to open at least 10 small accounts in the coming fiscal year. The salespeople focused on their goal, and with significant efforts, most were able to reach it. At the end of the year, they celebrated all the growth they had achieved—until the financials came in. For some reason, the profits had gone down. Upon further review, it was discovered that the smaller accounts consumed resources in several ways that were not immediately obvious. They did not pay bills on time; write-offs were higher; they did not produce their own artwork and consumed creative time that the publisher provided free as an inducement to "get them in the door"; and they often bought only one ad and waited to see if it produced results. On top of this, they tended to like to do business face-to-face, and that took more of the salesperson's time.

The way to do business profitably with this segment involved a very different pricing strategy. The publisher developed a program in which significant discounts were provided to the small retailers, under the following conditions:

- *All sales were done over the phone;*
- *Retailers had to buy at least six ads (this not only ensured that they had a better chance of getting results, but also that*

ads produced by the publisher's creative department generated sufficient revenue to w.arrant the effort);

- *They pre-paid by credit card.*

The program was a tremendous success. The publisher's costs went down and revenue skyrocketed. The retailers paid a lower price per ad and got better results from their advertising.

To ensure that the large national advertisers did not "bleed" into this program, the publisher built a price fence making the program available only for ads that were too small for the large retailers to even consider buying. But these ads were exactly the size that most local retailers wanted and expected to run.

Summary

There is no shame in operating at a strong Level 2. After all, a good cop is respected.

Here are some important things to keep in mind if you are to become effective at Level 2:

- The word "no" is critical to success.
- You will need to identify some "winners" and "losers" in your customer base, and re-price them accordingly.
- Good data and reliable list prices can make it or break it at Level 2. Bad data, on the other hand, will keep you firefighting at Level 1.
- Key tools are the Price Dispersion, Price Waterfall, and Variance Tree.
- Strategy is primarily cost-based, combined with some common sense; there is not a deep sense of value.

Once a company is highly effective at Level 2, the natural progression is to move to Level 3—that's next!

Level 3—
The Partner

The climb from Level 2 to Level 3 is a steep one.

At Level 2, a company's pricing processes are internally focused, often resulting in a cost-based approach to pricing. At Level 3, by contrast, the company begins to look externally and to take a value-based approach instead.

When we talk about value based-pricing, we could equally be referring to either of the two types of value: financial or perceived. Financial value is an economic measure, while perceived value takes into account such benefits as service, technical support, and brand.

Value-based pricing is driven by a deep understanding of the customer's perception of value, both financial and perceived. To ensure that deep customer knowledge is at the heart of pricing decision-making, a company must introduce a number of new processes that incorporate information from beyond the boundaries of the company's internal systems and "tribal knowledge."

The acquisition of this information requires formal development of the soft skills, such as listening, asking pertinent questions, using customer-focused tools, and investing in research and intelligence gathering that does not always yield precise answers.

If an organization is to progress from Level 2 to Level 3, it is critical that the sales team not be the only voice of the customer; there must be other credible information sources. If customer insight is purely anecdotal, there is a natural tendency to place undue emphasis on the most recent sales call or the squeakiest wheel.

Another challenge is to provide the sales team with effective sales tools that demonstrate the value of the product or service being sold. For example, value calculators that add up the net financial benefits that accrue from doing business with the company and demonstrate payback are essential in a B2B setting. We often say that confidence in the value proposition puts steel in the backbone of the sales force during negotiations. Developing a business case for the perceived value created by the offering may seem like a challenge, but it's one that top Level 3 firms take seriously. In many cases, convincing salespeople of the differential value of the company's offerings is as difficult as persuading the customer. Overcoming the notion that the sales team acts on behalf of the customer is a big part of the 18- to 36-month journey from Level 2 to Level 3.

Culture Shift: from "Policeman" to "Partner"

At Level 3, the pricing manager's role undergoes a dramatic transformation, from that of a "Policeman" to more of a "Partner."

Pricing managers move from what is often an antagonistic relationship with the sales force to one that is more like a teammate trying to solve a common problem. This entails a shift away from the role of saying "no" on a regular basis, to instead helping find creative ways to solve pricing problems and identify opportunities.

For pricing managers, change management is the critical skill at this stage of the journey. After all, you have to not only get senior management to buy in, but also gain the co-operation of Sales, Marketing, Finance, Operations, and a host of other functional areas to rally around customer value.

Ultimately, the Partner is able to tap into and leverage the knowledge and wisdom of the various functions in the organization. The sales, marketing, finance, operations, market research, and customer service teams can collectively provide a unique blend of insight and perspective into the company's value proposition, leading to more profitable pricing strategies that deliver long-term results.

- **Marketing** brings knowledge of how the product is used by customers, as well as segmentation, and value relative to the next-best alternative.
- **Finance** can provide valuable information about cost to serve and customer profitability.
- **Operations** can be integrated into the value chain to provide input into how customer feedback about the offering can be implemented effectively.
- **Customer Service** hears directly from customers about "value in use." Pricing managers who listen to an hour or two of calls into the call center or order desk every month are always rewarded with a high return on the effort expended.

From Rules to Insight

At Level 3, companies invest in research to ensure that customer insight replaces anecdotal information. This allows the pricing organization to spend less time enforcing rules and more time developing innovative ways for the organization to capture value.

We have seen great benefit when there is an opportunity for the functional leaders to share their knowledge, providing a more holistic view of the customer and leading to better pricing. Following a cross-functional summit focused on the value a company's offering delivers to customers, a client recently commented: "We have never before taken a day to talk about value from the customers' perspective, and its impact on pricing strategy. We have a great opportunity to leverage what we learned here today."

By making these kinds of investments, companies can price with a confidence gained through deep insight into the customer, rather than relying on "cost plus" tactics out of fear of losing volume and profit.

It is important to note that, at Level 3, we are not doing precision-based pricing focused on price elasticity—that will come in Level 4. Instead, we are engaged in "wisdom-based pricing," built on insight into the value the customer sees in your offering relative to that of its next-best alternative (the competition).

By sharing information across company functions, a common perception of the customer's needs develops, and a better understanding of the price/value relationship emerges.

To be effective in this endeavor, you need to build good relationships with highly respected salespeople in the organization who have demonstrated an ability to capture margin and volume. Having the most influential salespeople onside during the research and development of the Value Pricing Strategy will enable you to get the rest of the sales force on board much more easily during the implementation. One way to accomplish this is to involve them in any research you undertake. That will, first of all, ensure that the sales force has a stake in the research and will see value in it. Secondly, your research will be more effective because the sales team will provide input that will result in a better survey, interview or focus group.

Level 3 Processes

Figure 3.1

The Four Core Pricing Processes

P1 Develop Pricing Strategy	P2 Set Customer Net Prices	P3 Execute Pricing	P4 Manage Performance
☐ Conduct Industry Level Analysis ☐ Conduct Value Analysis ☐ Develop Price Structure ☐ Set Pricing Strategy ☐ Assess Viability of Strategy	☐ Finalize Customer Offerings ☐ Map Customers to Price Structure ☐ Establish Selling Guidelines and Design Waterfall ☐ Support Customer/ Account Management Process	☐ Communicate Price/ Value ☐ Obtain Approvals ☐ Manage Pricing Data ☐ Manage Transaction Leakages and Customer Investments	☐ Measure Performance ☐ Manage Performance ☐ Make Adjustments ☐ Manage and Control Pricing Process

At Level 2, the focus was on P3—Execute Pricing—and P4—Manage Performance. Now that those processes have been cleaned up, and good rules and performance measurement systems are in place, we can turn to the task of developing a pricing strategy. For us, that means pricing for value. This is done in processes P1—Develop Pricing Strategy—and P2—Set Customer Net Prices.

Companies face two key questions as they transition from Level 2 to Level 3 pricing strategies:

- Are there opportunities to capture more of the value we have created?
- Having reduced leakages, and generally taken bigger price increases as we moved through Level 2, are we nearing any pricing cliffs (inflection points in the demand curve where further price increases lead to disproportionately high losses in demand)?

We will introduce tools in this chapter that will help you answer these questions and lead your company to capture the benefits of improved profits and market share that are available to Level 3 organizations.

Value-based pricing entails superior knowledge of your customers' needs, and the ability of your company's offerings to deliver against those needs in a way that enables the right product, in the right situation, for the right price. In some cases, this might mean increased profits through higher prices with stable volume, and in other cases, it could be the opportunity to increase market share with minimal price erosion or competitive response. To capture these potential gains, you need detailed information about the customers' understanding of value. (In a B2B business, this means how they make more money using your offerings; and in a B2C business, it means how they increase their utility or perceived value through the use of your offerings.) You also need to know how to read the market conditions, using tools to help you determine when it is time to make your pricing moves.

No Level-Jumping!

Many companies try to skip Level 3 and proceed directly to Level 4. After all, with the amount of transaction data available today, it is possible to use software to run an optimization algorithm that leads to mathematically optimized prices and increased profits—at least in the short run. However, there are several problems with this approach.

First of all, this one-dimensional optimization deals with P2, which is focused on setting price. It does not deal with P1, which concentrates on developing strategy. As we said in the Introduction, having a great strategy that is well executed is of much more value than having a good strategy that is brilliantly executed. Therefore, your company's greatest leverage is in sorting out your pricing strategy at P1.

A case in point is the airline industry. Although airlines have sophisticated price-optimization software, they are often horribly unprofitable. Passengers complain frequently about airline prices. We would argue that one possible cause of this dissatisfaction is that most airlines do not understand value very well.

It's nice to have an optimization engine, but it's better to have a great pricing strategy.

Using Pricing Research

In order to gain the in-depth customer knowledge necessary to operate at Level 3, it is helpful to use pricing research—not the sophisticated optimization research like conjoint analysis that is integral to Level 4, but rather, more basic methods tuned to the needs of a pricing process, such as won/loss analysis, purchase intent, and financial value measurement.

For example, a chemical manufacturer that regularly bids on large contracts has implemented a simple, yet effective, process for won/loss analysis. Whenever the company loses a bid, it has an external consultant conduct an in-depth interview with the lost account. By using an external consultant, rather than the sales rep that lost the deal, to do the interview, the company is able to gain much richer insight into the causes of loss. That's because the customer will typically tell the salesperson that he or she lost because of price. Customers are motivated to do this for two reasons: they do not want to hurt the salesperson's feelings, and they are setting up the opportunity to get a lower price next time.

Research has proven that customers cite price as the reason for lost bids 70% of the time, whereas in reality, price is the cause of only about 30% of lost bids[2]. The ability to untangle what is really price-related and what is presented as price-driven but is in fact due to other reasons, is critical. When a neutral third party conducts the interview, the subtext of a negotiation is not present. Consequently, the customer is usually more honest, and provides more insight into his or her buying criteria, and why he or she chose a particular supplier.

One of the most important things to remember when conducting pricing research is to focus on the overall value proposition, of which price is only one piece. If you focus the conversation on price, the customer will immediately begin understating the value of the product or service, and overstating his/her price sensitivity. Instead, focus on the overall value and let the customer bring up price naturally as part of the discussion. If you are doing a quantitative study, it is permissible to ask about price—but only at the end of the survey after you have thoroughly discussed the overall value proposition.

We do this by using the questions in the survey to start the respondent thinking about the last buying occasion. We begin with questions like: "Have there been occasions in the past 12 months in which you sought out the technical support of the company? How would you rate the quality and timeliness of that interaction? How important is timely delivery of these inputs to the smooth operation of your business? What is the potential impact of late delivery?" Once the respondent has been given time to think about how much he or she values the offerings, and is led through the situations in which the value is created, the answer to a question about price will be much more reliable. In the absence of this approach, the importance of price as a buying criterion is easily overstated.

Not all research at Level 3 has to focus on pricing. Often, companies have other types of studies that are useful for understanding value, such as customer-satisfaction research, value-in-use research, usage and awareness research, focus groups, etc. Pricing managers can leverage these data sources to populate value maps (which we introduce later in the chapter) and build consensus around the value the company is delivering. That, in turn, enables the development of a value-based pricing strategy.

Some companies, though, do not have this sort of information available, and the idea of spending money to gather it seems foreign. In that case, it is important to build a consensus among senior management around the need for pricing research. It is often easiest to obtain funding for research into new products, as they are mission-critical to the future success of the business. Increasingly, however, we are finding that pricing managers in the B2B space are receiving the pricing research dollars they need to be successful at Level 3.

Having selected your supplier, you must execute the project. But first, address the following questions:

- Whom should you include in your sample? We typically advise including customers from key segments, so that you understand the needs and value for each group. You may also want to include lost customers and customers of the competition to ensure you are getting a view beyond your own customer base. It is important to have a sample size large enough to obtain statistically significant (or at least reliable) results in each segment when it comes to the design phase of the project.
- How do you define the customer? In many B2B businesses, there are multiple purchasers. They may include procurement, technical users, senior management, etc. In some cases, you will want to include all of them in your sample. However, that can be expensive, so it may be beneficial to do qualitative interviews with all the groups, but focus the quantitative research on one or two key participants in the buying process. The other benefit of initial qualitative research is that it can help prioritize the issues from a customer perspective, and therefore provide focus for the quantitative study that follows.

The output from the research should be a deeper understanding of value (financial and/or perceived) and how much the customer is willing to pay.

Last but not least. When designing the research, it is important to include the various functional areas. We have consistently found that, if you do not include senior management, sales, finance, customer service, operations and other functions up front, they will tend to be resistant to the findings and ask many questions at the end that, at best, slow down the process and, at worst, derail it. The unique perspectives that each brings will add value to the design, while gaining their cooperation and support up front will save time in the long run.

Case study: Reaping the Rewards of Research

A former sales rep, Carol had been a pricing manager for several years. She was respected within the organization for her experience and tough-mindedness when it came to pricing, and senior management relied heavily on her. But the sales force saw her as a "Policeman" more than a Partner, and tried to work around her whenever possible. They disliked dealing with her because, when their opinions clashed, she tended to have the support of senior management.

Carol wanted to elevate the discussion, and was keen to move beyond enforcement into partnering with the sales team. She set out to do just that by attending pricing conferences and exposing her management team to what she had learned. Over time, she built a consensus from the management team that investing in better information would lead to better decisions and generate a healthier return. Carol obtained approval to undertake a pricing research and analytics initiative to gather fact-based customer information that would help improve the organization's pricing. She seized the opportunity, and engaged key managers and reps from the sales team in the process of designing the research and setting objectives and priorities for the insights they needed the research to deliver.

In addition, we made sure in designing the study that the questions were relevant to respondents from different segments. Questions that respondents don't feel are relevant will lead to abandoned surveys, or worse, misleading results.

When the results came in, there were many surprises for everyone, including Carol. It became evident that some core products were underpriced, and that there were several opportunities for using bundling to achieve more effective price segmentation. She shared this information with the sales team, and conducted strategy sessions to gain buy-in on how to apply it.

As the project moved from analysis and recommendations to implementation, Carol ended up with a robust new pricing strategy that the sales team would never have accepted if she had simply run the project as a pricing/finance/IT initiative that had the support of senior management.

But having the right strategy does not guarantee success. In the case of Carol's company, the sales force needed to break old habits of discounting and apologizing for the prices of the organization's offerings, rather than standing behind their value. Therefore, Carol invested in training for the sales force on how to execute the new pricing strategy, using insights into the value that the research had delivered. As a result, the sales team was able to implement the new strategy with alacrity.

Carol had boosted their confidence, and she had truly become a Partner.

During the implementation, she stayed involved; the sales team and other functional areas sought her out when problems arose because of her ability to bring facts and insights that led to superior business results. In a down economy, the business grew and outperformed its competitors by a significant margin.

Needs-based Segmentation

Segmentation at Level 2 tends to be based on classification, whereas at Level 3, it is according to need.

For example, companies at Level 2 typically segment customers based on traditional classifications, such as account size, region, and industry. Level 3 companies, however, move beyond these traditional classifications to needs-based segmentation—e.g., what needs differentiate one group of customers from another? *(See Figure 3.2 for an example of the difference when segmenting the dog market.)*

Figure 3.2

Classification versus Segmentation

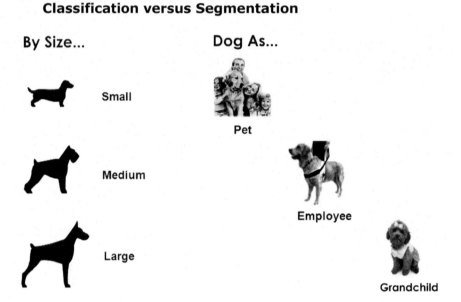

By Size...

Small

Medium

Large

Dog As...

Pet

Employee

Grandchild

A huge benefit of needs-based segmentation is the fact that it is customer-driven. By designing the value proposition around the customers' needs, the seller aligns with the buyer, making negotiations much smoother.

When the segmentation is classification-based, however, the sales force will struggle with execution because the pricing strategy does not relate directly to their customers' needs. Consequently, salespeople get "creative," finding ways to alter the pricing structure to fit those needs.

Offer Design

One of the keys to success in making the transition from Level 2 to Level 3 is the ability to connect P1—Develop Pricing Strategy—to P2—Set Customer Net Prices. This connection occurs in the process of Offer Design: the company takes what it knows about customer segmentation, current customer behavior, business objectives, and operational execution to develop a set of offers designed to maximize profits. There are some important concepts—and often many variables—to consider.

In Level 2, we introduced the concept of "Pricing along the demand curve." In Level 3, there is a lot more intelligence that can go into the design of the price fences (what should be included in a premium offer and what can be stripped out to create a basic offer). Cluster analysis of research results will identify the elements of the offer that are of high value to each segment. The following case study explains how one company used this knowledge to create offers that appealed to the unique needs of the different customer segments.

Having distinct customer offerings can remove much of the tension from the sales process. Instead of allowing the sales force to simply cut the price to win a deal, an effective Offer Design allows customers to self-select the distinct offer that best fits their needs, and balance price with the key elements you have included in your design.

Case study: Feed the Need

A construction-products company that sold through distribution found its margins slipping and customers becoming disgruntled with its inability to deliver on time. The company invested in research and discovered, much to its surprise, that customers fell into three key needs-based segments: Overall Performance-Driven, Delivery-Driven, and Price-Driven.

Therefore, the company built a price structure for each of these segments (see Table 3.1). As a result, share, margin, and profits all grew dramatically, almost immediately. The price structure had a second dimension that outlined the discount available to customers as they spent more money with the company. Having a well-designed offering, the sales team was better able to "stick to the script," and explain that customers would need to either pay more or do more business with the company in order to take advantage of the Platinum offerings that had previously simply been given away.

Table 3.1

Segment, Need, Strategy

Segment	Need	Strategy
Overall Performance-Driven	Certainty of delivery time, complete shipments, strong techical support	Create "Platinum" program for these customers, enabling them to commit high share of wallet for superior performance on the key value drivers
Delivery-Driven	Certainty of delivery time	Enable customers to choose delivery time, and provide guarantee for premium price
Price-Driven	Low price	No technical support and longer delivery lead times for substantially reduced prices

An added benefit of the program was that Operations loved it. Previously, all customers had been classified as "priority." The production schedule changed daily, meaning that, in the end, no customers received product on time. Segmenting customers according to need, on the other hand, provided a tremendous opportunity to deliver superior value (as defined by customers) and, in turn, capture higher margins.

But in order to make it happen, the process must first be activated with high-quality information about what customers value. Before an organization can introduce value-based pricing, it needs to become more disciplined in its definition and measurement of value. Often, value is not managed in a structured way, but is instead maintained as a "mental model" in the heads of a few individuals. To improve the management of value, the organization must also improve the quality of the models used to describe and measure it. To facilitate this, we are introducing two key tools for Level 3.

The Perceived Value Map

Perceived value is the soft value or, to use a concept borrowed from economics, "utility" attached to a product. It is not easily quantified, but can make a huge difference to the customer's buying decision. For example, when buying a car, you may consider attributes like brand, comfort, and performance, which are not economic factors but are extremely important nonetheless.

There is an excellent tool, called the Perceived Value Map (PVM), to help you quantify perceived value. In a nutshell, it integrates the wisdom of the organization's personnel, links it to price, and places it in a model that can be communicated, debated, and tracked over time. You can also use this tool as a way to leverage and compare insights from market research.

The value map creates a context for understanding relative value, which we define as the quality delivered for the price paid (Q/P). The output or model leads to more productive discussions, and helps you identify what you don't know and what information you need to obtain.

Table 3.2

Seven-Step Value Map Process

Step	Process
1	Define the customer segment
2	Weight the importance of price versus benefits
3	Identify and define the attributes (buying criteria) that will be used to evaluate the alternatives
4	Weight the attributes/criteria
5	Score yourself relative to the competition on a scale of 1-10
6	Input prices for your offering and that of your competitors
7	Review value map

Once you have completed this process, you will have a picture like *Figure 3.3*.

Figure 3.3

Customer Value Map

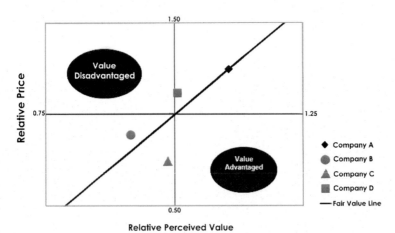

Here, we have drawn a value map. The map has two axes. The "y" axis is relative price, with higher prices shown further up the axis. The "x" axis is perceived value—the further to the right, the more value you are providing from the customers' perspective.

The line sloping upwards is the Fair Value Line—anywhere along the line, value is equivalent and customers are relatively indifferent. In other words, it is a fair tradeoff between price and value. (In step 1, remember, we advised selection of a segment of customers. With the proper selection of a segment, it is valid to assume that fair value is represented by a straight line.) If your offering falls below the Fair Value Line, it is "value advantaged"; if it is above the line, it is "value disadvantaged"—you are providing less value for the price than the competition is. (In this case, "B" and "D" are value disadvantaged, "C" is value advantaged, and "A" is a fair value.)

The slope of the Fair Value Line relates to the rate at which customers trade off price and value. For price-sensitive segments, the line is flat—you have to provide significant value to be rewarded with a higher price. Conversely, for price-insensitive segments, the slope is very steep; a small increase in value provides a good opportunity to capture a higher price.

The value map is an effective tool for organizations because it can be implemented at four distinct levels of proficiency:

1. By yourself to create a simple view of the customer, segment, or market;
2. With a cross-functional team internally to validate and document assumptions and build the consensus view;
3. With the direct input of a relatively small number of customers, or by re-purposing existing research that contains information that can be re-framed as an input to the value map;
4. With a statistically significant sample of customers in a formal research process.

The quality of the output improves with a move to the next higher level of proficiency, but the basic value map remains the same. This allows for validation of assumptions, and the ability to challenge some of the company folklore and biases about customer perception.

The value map becomes more precise as you include customer input or past research you have undertaken (e.g., segmentation, customer satisfaction, etc.). You can assess its accuracy by cross-referencing the position on the map with recent results. If you are value advantaged, your market share should be growing; if you are value disadvantaged, your share should be shrinking. If either condition is false, your value map is inaccurate, and the weighting, scoring, or segmentation needs to be adjusted.

The value map is an important tool for Level 3 because of its versatility. It works in nearly every situation, and has been used effectively to look at the overall market, customer segments, and individual customer purchases during a key account process. In fact, the only instance where we have not found the Perceived Value Map to be highly useful is in monopolistic markets where the pricing questions are more about fairness than value.

Case study: B2B Manufacturer

The president of a B2B manufacturing company wanted to take a price increase on a key product, but was getting strong resistance from the sales force. He was confident that the product's brand name and superior ease of use were reason enough to capture the increased price, but he needed to get the sales team onside.

To do so, he convened a meeting to train the sales force on value-based pricing, including the preparation of value maps. The results of that exercise clearly indicated that the company was value advantaged in many different segments, and could command a premium price. Armed with that information, the sales team had the confidence to sell the product at the higher price. Even though this exercise was done at a proficiency Level 2, the exercise had created a consensus view that gave the sales team confidence.

Financial Value Measurement

Financial Value Measurement (FVM) is the tool we use to build a model of the financial value that your offering provides to customers relative to their next-best alternative. Financial value is achieved in one of four ways: lower operating cost, higher productivity, reduced asset base, or reduced risk *(see Figure 3.4)*.

Figure 3.4

Financial Value Measurement (FVM)

- **Lower operating cost**—your offering enables the customer to reduce business costs. For example, your route optimization software allows a courier company to improve the efficiency of the pick-up schedule by 15%.
- **Higher productivity**—the customer can obtain more output through the same asset base, increasing capacity and revenue. For example, an improved fertilizer that increases the yield of corn on an acre of land.
- **Reduced asset base**—the customer can reduce its investment in fixed assets or inventory. For example,

just-in-time delivery means the customer can reduce the number of parts in inventory.

- **Reduced risk**—the customer experiences lower levels of risk. For example, a well-designed preventative maintenance program reduces the risk of catastrophic failure by 50%.

Understanding your financial value, and providing the sales force with facts that have been built into an FVM calculator significantly enhances your ability to capture value.

FVM is a process that many companies shy away from because they think that it is too difficult to build with accuracy, and that customers will be unwilling to share data necessary for its development or to accept its outputs. However, there is no question that in B2B settings, customers make decisions to maximize their long-term profits. Without knowing how your offering impacts customer profitability and return on assets, you will be destined to struggle with Level 3.

The first challenge is gaining access to customer data. Customers are concerned that anything you learn will be used against them. To break into the realm of FVMs, you may need a launch customer to whom you can offer an incentive to provide test data. But that isn't the only way. Often, when your product fails in the field, the customer starts sharing reams of key data that you can use in your FVM tool. Unfortunately, most organizations are not tuned in to hear the information at this time of crisis: "Do you realize that every hour that line is down it costs us $10,000?" "We make 40,000 parts an hour on that line, and when you deliver off-spec material, it slows our line down by 20%—and that's after we spend an hour re-setting the dials." "If one of your cracked parts gets into the field, our tech support team has to deal with the problem. That will cost 10 times as much to fix the problem, and that's not including the damage to the other components." Maybe that customer is too far gone to save, but this information can have tremendous value in building an FVM for other customers.

Assessing Financial Value

As you develop an FVM calculator, keep in mind that customers assess the financial value in three ways:

- What is the **size** of the financial benefit?
- How **certain** am I we will realize that benefit?
- How **fast** will we realize those benefits?

Size, certainty, and speed—of the three, certainty is the most important criterion. In other words, customers want a "check they can cash."

A fatal flaw that many companies make is focusing on the potential size of the benefits, rather than the certainty.

To illustrate, imagine you can choose one of the following two options:

- A lottery ticket with a $2-million payout and a 70% chance of winning; or
- A lottery ticket with a $1-million payout and a 95% chance of winning.

Which would you choose? Over the years, we have asked this in hundreds of seminars, and the overwhelming response is the $1-million ticket, even though the average expected payout is much less than the $2-million ticket ($1 million x 95% = $0.95 million expected value versus $2 million x 70% = $1.4 million expected value).

Most people want the certainty of a payout, and customers are no different.

Now let's take it a step further and turn it into a pricing question: How much of your own money would you pay for the $2-million ticket, and how much would you pay for the $1-million ticket?

Once again, most people would pay significantly more for the $1-million ticket because of the certainty.

The lesson: In designing the offer, building in elements that create certainty provide the opportunity for higher price realization. We do this by supporting claims with field trials, offering warrantees, or designing a price structure that is built around pay for performance.

Case study: Banking on an FVM

A bank was launching a Web-based banking product for its small and mid-sized business customers. It developed an FVM demonstrating the financial value of Internet banking that increased productivity and lowered operating costs.

The impact of this simple tool was dramatic. During most product launches, the sales team requested discounts for 90% of all deals. In this case, however, they requested discounts for only 20% of the deals that they signed. The v.p. of marketing was very surprised, and admitted somewhat sheepishly: "I always thought the problem was that our sales team could not sell value. This exercise helped me realize that, if we provide them with the right tools, they can—and will—sell the value and capture the prices we are after."

Providing Pricing Guidance with the 5Cs

The 5Cs of pricing—costs, competition, capacity, conditions, and customer—are like ingredients for a recipe. If you use them wisely, you will prepare a delicious dish—i.e., pricing strategy. We use the 5Cs to help understand the structure and health of the market. The value map might indicate that you are highly value advantaged, but in a market where customers are going bankrupt and your product represents 50% of their cost structure (or your service is a luxury and consumers don't have jobs), the 5Cs will tell you loud and clear that this is not the right time to be thinking about a price increase.

We will comment briefly on costs, competition, capacity, conditions, and customers. At the end of this section, we will show you a tool that can help integrate all of the 5Cs into a cohesive whole for decision-making purposes.

Costs: Insight into costs is critical to ensuring profitability. This knowledge does not necessarily tell you how to price, but it does set a price floor that you cannot go below on a consistent basis without going out of business.

The key to using your cost information wisely is to marry it with customer insight. For example, if the cost to serve different customers varies widely, you may be able to combine that with customer insight to develop unique offerings that are highly competitive and, at the same time, help you deal with inadequate profitability.

It is also important to understand the changes that you (and your competitors) can expect to see in the cost structure of the business. While we don't advocate presenting a price increase to a customer based on a cost argument (because when the cost trend reverses, the customer will ask you to back out the cost increase), knowing when there may be some headwinds or tailwinds to your pricing strategy can be really beneficial. In early 2008, for example, many states in the U.S. introduced significant increases to the minimum wage. For many retail companies, this offered a free pass to increase prices without facing a backlash. Also, by understanding cost trends, you can predict when the industry leaders will be more likely to take a price increase; if your strategy is to be a fast follower, you can implement quickly.

Case study: Calculating the Cost to Serve

A financial-services client suspected that some customers were unprofitable. It conducted a cost-to-serve analysis to build a customer profitability model. The company thought that because it had a low variable cost, any business was profitable.

But it discovered that small customers were consuming a disproportionate amount of resources (account rep time, customer-service support, high turnover, bad debts, etc.). It also learned that small customers were typically a younger demographic, and that they preferred to interact electronically when possible. With a proper cost-to-serve analysis, the company reconfigured its service offering with small accounts by shifting the selling and support effort to the Web. The impact was immediate; profits and service improved, while costs went down.

Competition: Customers evaluate all offers versus their next-best alternative. Therefore, understanding your competition is critical to understanding your value in the marketplace. Furthermore, the pricing decisions that you make affect your competitors, and can lead to unintended consequences, such as price wars. Competitive intelligence will help you forecast the impact of your pricing actions on your competitors' business, and thereby develop a successful strategy.

Some fundamental questions to ask: How might this pricing action affect our competitors? How might they react? If you have the insight to answer these questions, you will have a better chance of developing a pricing strategy that will build your business for the long term. Remember the words of ancient Chinese military strategist Sun Tzu: "The best thing of all is to take the enemy's country whole and intact; to shatter and destroy it is not so good."

Case study: Keeping an Eye on Competitors

A pharmaceutical company specializing in animal health had developed an innovative new drug. It commissioned a market-research study to determine the pricing strategy. Based on the results, the optimal price in the short run was $11.50. However, the company believed that if it were to charge that price, it would take so much market share from its competitors that it would cause a price war, thereby diminishing the positive impact of the $11.50 price point. At $13.00, the pharma company forecasted its profits *to be slightly less in the short term, but predicted the competition would not react. The company priced at $13.00 and, as expected, the competition did not react.*

The next year, the pharma company raised its price from $13.00 to $14.00. The competition followed with a price increase, thus raising the overall profitability of the market (see Figures 3.5 and 3.6).

Figure 3.5
Customer Value Map

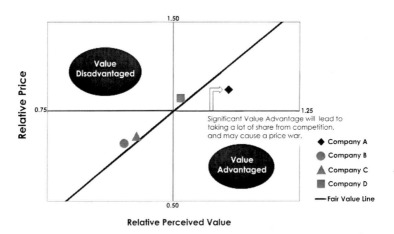

Figure 3.6
Customer Value Map

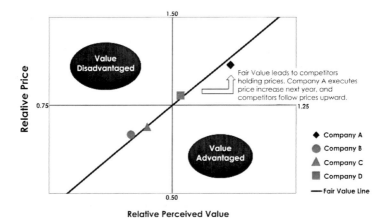

Capacity: In some industries (especially those in which the product is tending towards the commodity end of the spectrum), capacity utilization is the single greatest driver of price. If there is oversupply, prices fall; if there is under-capacity, prices rise. Industries that are driven by capacity, such as chemicals and oil, often have highly accurate forecasts that they use to help them project price trends based on capacity utilization.

But other businesses do not track this important lever carefully enough, and as a result, are not aware of the leverage they have either gained or lost.

Case study: Caught Napping in Capacity Crunch

A client in the tire business had been operating at overcapacity for years and, as a result, had very little pricing power during that time. Eventually, however, the environment changed; as the market grew and no new manufacturing capacity was added, the company found itself with more demand than it could fulfill. But because it had not tracked capacity closely, the company had already locked itself into long-term contracts that did not allow it to take advantage of this change in circumstances.

Conditions: Macro-economic trends impact pricing. During recessions, most companies sell less and prices tend to go down. The opposite is true when the economy is robust and growing.

Forecasting economic trends is a significant area of endeavor for many think-tanks and financial institutions. We have many clients who have identified a few key economic indicators that are relevant to their industry (e.g., housing starts for the construction industry, consumer confidence for retail, etc.). The point here is not to be exhaustive, but to ensure you include conditions as a factor in the overall pricing strategy, and have contingency plans in place should conditions change.

Case study: Changing Prices with Conditions

A passenger-train company tracks the price of retail gas to predict changes in demand. The model it has built is predictive within a range of +-5%. The company knows that when there are spikes in the price of gas, demand for its services goes up. When there are declines in gas prices, demand goes down, particularly in major corridors.

The company experiences variations in demand of as much as 20%, and is able to adjust its prices accordingly. When it starts to hit capacity, it raises its prices.

Customer: The key difference between Levels 2 and 3 is the depth of customer insight that companies have when they make pricing decisions. Level 2 companies are primarily cost-based pricers, and customer insight is not essential to that process. Level 3 companies, on the other hand, are value-based pricers, and such knowledge is central to effective pricing decisions.

Earlier in the chapter, we introduced the Perceived Value Map and Financial Value Measurement as models that can be used to measure the value of your company's offerings relative to the customer's next-best alternative.

While these are important tools in the customer area of our model, it is also advisable to think about the financial health of your customer when designing your strategy and determining your next pricing move. For example, ask yourself questions like: How important is my offering to my customer (in financial or emotional terms)? How profitable is my customer, and how has that been changing? What macro trends are my customers facing? Are there substitute products or alternative solutions that could render my product obsolete? How many customers are in the market? Your pricing strategy will differ markedly for a business with five major customers, compared with a B2C business.

Building a 5Cs Dashboard

An effective way to manage the price-setting process is to build a 5Cs dashboard. A good dashboard has several indicators that measure whether a company should increase or decrease prices. The specifics will vary, but the foundation remains basically the same. The advantage of a dashboard is that it is an agreed-upon, objective measure that removes the emotion.

Table 3.3

The 5Cs

C	Description
Costs	How are costs changing? Are they going up? How much?
Customer	What is the strength of our relative value proposition? Are we value-advantaged or value-disadvantaged? How is it changing?
Competition	Are competitors raising prices? What changes in market share are happening versus the competition?
Capacity	How high is capacity utilization, for our company and our industry?
Conditions	Is the economy getting stronger or weaker? How are sales in our industry? Are there leading or lagging indicators that provide insight?

A weighting is applied to each of the Cs, and they are scored as to whether the trends are positive or negative. This provides an overall score. For example, a 1/5 would indicate it is a poor time for a price increase, while a 4/5 would signify the opposite.

Case study: Automotive Parts Firm

Historically, price increases at this organization were taken either when costs increased or when there was a need to "fill a hole in the P&L"—in other words, for internally driven reasons!

The company developed a pricing dashboard, and it quickly moved the discussion away from internally driven needs to achieving a better understanding of the market and the tradeoffs between price and volume. Over the years, the company refined the dashboard, and it is now a central process to the successful ongoing management of pricing.

Figure 3.7

Strategic Pricing Recommendations – Forecast Period: CALENDAR YEAR

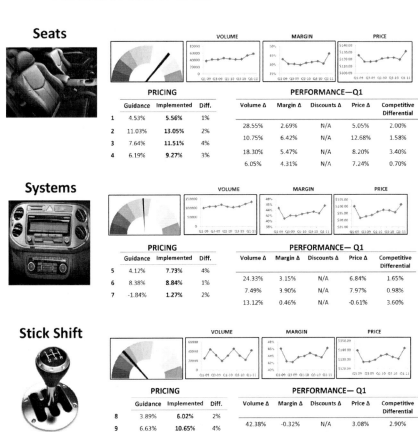

Seats

	PRICING		
	Guidance	Implemented	Diff.
1	4.53%	5.56%	1%
2	11.03%	13.05%	2%
3	7.64%	11.51%	4%
4	6.19%	9.27%	3%

PERFORMANCE—Q1				
Volume Δ	Margin Δ	Discounts Δ	Price Δ	Competitive Differential
28.55%	2.69%	N/A	5.05%	2.00%
10.75%	6.42%	N/A	12.68%	1.58%
18.30%	5.47%	N/A	8.20%	3.40%
6.05%	4.31%	N/A	7.24%	0.70%

Systems

	PRICING		
	Guidance	Implemented	Diff.
5	4.12%	7.73%	4%
6	8.38%	8.84%	1%
7	-1.84%	1.27%	2%

PERFORMANCE— Q1				
Volume Δ	Margin Δ	Discounts Δ	Price Δ	Competitive Differential
24.33%	3.15%	N/A	6.84%	1.65%
7.49%	3.90%	N/A	7.97%	0.98%
13.12%	0.46%	N/A	-0.61%	3.60%

Stick Shift

	PRICING		
	Guidance	Implemented	Diff.
8	3.89%	6.02%	2%
9	6.63%	10.65%	4%

PERFORMANCE— Q1				
Volume Δ	Margin Δ	Discounts Δ	Price Δ	Competitive Differential
42.38%	-0.32%	N/A	3.08%	2.90%
15.74%	4.88%	N/A	8.49%	3.40%

Summing up the 5Cs

A good question to ask in evaluating your pricing strategy is: "What is the quality of our organization's insight into the 5Cs?"

Our experience is that when you have high-quality insight into each of the 5Cs, the pricing strategy is both obvious and elegant, and rarely complicated. But if you have limited insight, everything is difficult because you simply don't have the data you need to make decisions that everyone can rally around—and that leads to stress, disagreement, and turf battles over who knows best.

The key to a successful strategy is to have good processes connected to each of the 5Cs:

- What is the quality of your information-gathering for each of the 5Cs?
- What one piece of information for each "C" would most highly leverage your ability to formulate an effective pricing strategy?

Level 3 Pricing Strategies

In this section, we provide examples of some of the pricing strategies that are commonly deployed by Level 3 organizations.

Design to Price

The drama goes like this. Product Development creates a new product. The cost of the new product is higher than expected. The company adds an "acceptable" margin to this higher-than-expected cost, which leads to a higher-than-acceptable price. The sales force believes the product is too high-priced, but the company asks them to sell it anyway. Surprise, surprise—the feedback from customers is that it is too expensive. The result: the company must lower the price, and now the product-development team is back at the drawing board trying to figure out how to take out costs!

The product-development process at most companies is flawed, working as follows:

Product→ Cost → Price → Value → Customer

Many companies are counteracting this common problem by introducing staged gate processes that are much more rigorous at weeding out the losers, or designing out unnecessary elements of the offering earlier in the product-development process.

One of the key changes is to include in-depth pricing research at a much earlier stage of product development. Companies are trying to gain a much deeper understanding of the price/value tradeoff earlier in the process, to determine whether it is justified to move to the next stage of investment. The goal is to kill bad ideas more quickly, and nurture good ones.

When this process is executed at a world-class level, it is referred to as "design to price," and works as follows:

Customer → Value → Price → Cost →Product

In this process, the customer is the focal point, and price comes *before* cost.

Here's how it works. Once you know the value, you can estimate what the customer is willing to pay. And once you know what the potential price is, you can determine what the cost must be to make this an attractive product to develop. If you can develop the product for that cost, it is a go; if not, it either gets killed or more value must be created to enable the company to charge a higher price.

Case study: Home Furnishings Designed to Price

One company that has implemented the "design to price" philosophy with alacrity is IKEA. In fact, IKEA is so proud of its process that it actually advertises it!

Figure 3.8

The final stage of the new product pricing process is setting the go-to-market price. At this stage, many companies engage in in-depth pricing optimization research to help them be much more precise in determining the optimal price. We will discuss this in the next chapter.

Price Structure

One of the most tangible benefits of understanding how the customer realizes value is the opportunity to create highly innovative pricing structures.

In B2B, most companies are negotiating with Procurement during at least part of the selling process. The procurement department specializes in commoditizing products (by declaring there is no differentiation in the market), and shifting the negotiation away from value and onto costs, if it is advantageous for it to do so. For companies that do not thoroughly understand the value of their offering, this creates a situation in which they are very likely going to leave a lot of money on the table.

But once a company does understand the value, it is in a much better position to price for it. This does not mean that Procurement will make it any easier, but it does open the door to developing innovative pricing structures that enable the company to reposition the product and change the conversation with that department.

Case study: Hospital Bed Manufacturer

A manufacturer of hospital beds had developed a superior product that made it easier to lift and move patients. The manufacturer conducted a study to determine the bed's impact on workers' compensation costs due to fewer back injuries and lower employee absenteeism.

The study revealed a substantial reduction in workers' compensation claims. Therefore, the manufacturer priced the bed at a significant premium, at which Procurement initially balked. But here's the kicker: the manufacturer guaranteed the reduction in workers' compensation claims; if the savings were not realized, the bed could be returned for a full refund. This enabled the company to charge up to 50% more for its bed versus the next-best alternative, even though the cost of production was only marginally higher.

Currently, many companies are transitioning their products to software as a service (SaaS). This is a massive change in delivery, and requires the development of recurring revenue models and a move away from equipment purchases.

This presents both an opportunity and a threat. Most companies are in the process of making this change, and it is too early to say whether or not it has been a success. But our observation is that the companies that have the greatest chance of success are investing heavily in customer research to ensure they understand the value they will deliver under the SaaS model.

Case study: Telecommunications Company

A telecommunications company that sells trading systems to brokers/dealers developed an SaaS offer on the cloud. Historically, it had sold telecommunications equipment that was located on the client's site. It had a very limited view of the customers' perspective on this new initiative, and invested in doing research to gain insight.

The company discovered that there were different customer segments; some were open to SaaS, while others preferred the existing model. Additionally, it gained insight into the tradeoff customers made between these two solutions and price. The company is working through the challenges of developing a completely new product and pricing structure armed with deep customer insight that enables it to move swiftly and with confidence.

Finding the Cliff in the Demand Curve

One of the most important benefits of moving to Level 3 from Level 2 is the ability to determine when an aggressive pricing strategy is allowing you to capture more value, and when it is taking you to the edge of a cliff. In Level 2, we introduced a company that was World Class at Level 2. It was becoming uncomfortable with all the price increases it had taken, and came to us wondering if it was at the precipice of the cliff. It had no information on value, and had simply been raising prices to improve the health of its P&L.

In fact, we see this approach of using pricing to plug a gap on the P&L so frequently that we have developed a name for it: **"The Jaws of Pricing."** As you look at the next diagram you will see why-as price goes up, volume goes down, and vice-versa.

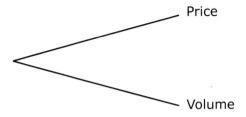

Price

Volume

The problem arises when the business loses sight of value. But how do you know when you are approaching the cliff? There is no single answer, but a long history of opening the jaws of pricing is one indicator; a shrinking customer base is another; and being value disadvantaged on the PVM is a third.

One other analysis, however, we found to be quite interesting. Our client was a national manufacturer that served a broad base of other manufacturing companies in the country. Its product wasn't a huge input cost for its customers, and it had been taking some very healthy price increases over the past few years. As we thought about the potential cliff ahead, we looked at whether its customers were moving production to other plants in the region. When we saw that this was the case, we took it as a sign that possibly the company had gone too far, and that customers had moved production to cheaper locales.

Pricing Infrastructure

We identified the changing role for the pricing organization at the start of this chapter. Our belief is that, if you modify any one of the elements in the pricing infrastructure, others will need to change accordingly to restore its fit and balance as your company progresses to the next level.

Here are some of the infrastructure considerations for companies moving to Level 3.

Structure: At Level 3, the pricing department is typically best suited to report in to Marketing. Finance is focused on costs and controls, but has no insight into customers. If Pricing is to gain buy-in as a Partner, it must build customer knowledge by partnering with market research and competitive intelligence, if those departments exist at the company. The slight against the marketing department is that it is often disconnected from the market price (there are many businesses who take a big price increase each year only to deal most or all of it back in the form of discounts, rebates etc.). For the pricing department located in Marketing, the challenge is to remain connected to the market by building strong relationships with the sales department.

People: Advancing from Level 2 to Level 3 typically requires an investment in people. For example, a move from across-the-board price increases to a more strategic approach necessitates an investment in understanding value and helping the sales force implement this approach to selling. This means there may be a need for additional resources in the pricing department and in sales training. Note: It is extremely beneficial at this level to have a former salesperson on your team; this will help achieve sales buy-in.

The management style at Level 3 is collaborative, focused on collective problem-solving. Your people are change agents more than data crunchers. If you have a team of analysts, training in change management is critical.

At Level 3, the pricing team must get out of the office and establish effective contacts, earn trust, and maybe even participate in sales calls.

Moving to Level 3 takes courage. Often, it leads to turnover in the sales team, as some salespeople cannot make the adjustment from chasing volume to managing profit. Once our clients have gone through the process, they always say: "The loss of these people was a blessed event."

Systems: The software and systems available today do a far better job in supporting Level 2 (with tools for measurement and control) and Level 4 (with optimization algorithms) than Level 3. Level 3 is about value—that kind of information typically exists outside the company and is therefore harder to capture in a piece of software.

Tools such as Sharepoint and Business Intelligence systems are rapidly being adopted as central repositories for corporate knowledge. Using this technology to document Financial Value Measurement (FVM) case studies, store the results and findings of market-research studies, or outline the process and necessary data for creating an effective value story with customers (by segment) is an effective way to enable the Level 3 processes.

We also introduced the Perceived Value Map (PVM) tool. While many companies manage this process using simple Excel spreadsheets, that system presents a high degree of risk that knowledge will be lost when key managers change jobs. We advocate that this important information be properly stored and maintained so the evolution of value can be managed over time.

Results: At Level 3, companies take a more balanced view of share and margin. They are looking for the sweet spot, and are willing, albeit grudgingly, to sacrifice at least some volume for the sake of profit.

Key performance indicators are critical to ensuring that the strategy is supporting the objectives. For example, one transportation company found that there was a direct link between a monthly value index it used to measure customer satisfaction, and price and market share.

Paying the Sales Force for Margin

Another important change at Level 3 is sales-force compensation. At Level 2, organizations primarily reward salespeople for delivering either volume or revenue. At Level 3, however, this does not work; a significant proportion of sales compensation must transition to metrics that can be shown to drive margin improvement. This gets salespeople aligned with overall pricing objectives of maximizing profits, not just revenue, and creates further alignment and support for the pricing manager in his or her journey to becoming the Partner. The reason revenue/volume as the primary focus doesn't work is because the easiest way to grow either one is by cutting the price. At Level 3, the emphasis must be on selling value. The only way to ensure that happens is to focus the sales force on margin, so they share in the rewards of enhancing the company's profitability.

In our experience, most companies undergo a radical transformation when they make margin or profit improvement a significant proportion of sales-force compensation. With a revenue- or volume-based program, we find the sales team typically expends more effort negotiating internally than externally. But once the shift has been made to a margin- or profit-based program, this situation changes dramatically, with the sales team becoming much more focused on negotiating with customers, and less focused on negotiating internally for increased discounts.

In decentralized businesses, companies often use total gross margin as the main driver of the variable compensation plan. But upon a deeper review of the transaction records in these businesses, we often see large deals in which the price has been cut dramatically. However, because they still generate positive margin, the general manager has lobbied hard for their approval. The balance between simplicity and effectiveness can be tricky to attain, but rewarding people for price or rate improvement, growth, and mix improvement is also an objective in the transition to a Level 3 pricing company.

Process: At Level 3, we are focused primarily on P1—the 5Cs, needs-based segmentation, and developing pricing strategy; and P2—developing a price structure that allows the organization to adjust the offering to varying price levels.

Summary

At Level 3, the successful pricing manager assumes the role of Partner. He or she must be able to manage change and facilitate meetings in which multiple perspectives are provided. In particular, he or she must be able to bring the sales force on board, finding the salespeople who embody value-based selling and gaining their trust. Having an ex-salesperson on the team can be very helpful.

The word "no" has been replaced by discussions about value and price.

The customer is the focal point. Objective, fact-based insight into the customer is critical to ensure the playing field is level and no function has an unfair advantage. Companies at Level 3 conduct research to acquire customer data that everyone can rally around.

Level 4—
The Scientist

We call Level 4 "the Scientist" because at this stage, companies leverage the science of pricing to make better, faster decisions than their competitors.

The predominant theme at Level 4 is optimization, and we will focus most of the chapter on that topic.

Price optimization is a methodology that helps a company maximize the tradeoffs that customers are likely to make between the offering, its price, and the expected volume so it can achieve its goals. The actual focus of the optimization may be margin or profit, volume or market share, or some combination thereof. Whatever the ultimate goal, price optimization involves understanding the relationship between changes in the offering and changes in demand, and finding the optimal combination. The definition of price optimization in B2C is relatively straightforward, but we have been careful with our explanation here because in B2B, the demand curve is often an elusive concept. However, we can still use price optimization techniques to evaluate the various tradeoffs that customers make.

In a B2B context, this typically focuses on one of four areas:

- The optimal price for new products, thus ensuring that money is not left on the table;
- Deal optimization—the sales force has a tool that provides pricing guidance for a specific deal, often built off of micro-segmentation (more on that later);
- Maximizing the tradeoff between price and volume in a capacity-constrained industry (e.g., petrochemicals);
- Optimizing the likelihood of customers upgrading to the next model, or selecting a particular product option or feature as prices or price gaps change.

In B2C and B2B2C, price optimization is often more easily applied due to the availability of more comprehensive data that is not tainted by the complexities of sales cycles, business relationships, technical specifications, etc. Therefore, in many B2C industries, there is intense focus on understanding consumer needs and perceptions. For example, the consumer packaged goods (CPG) industry has access to sophisticated data such as store-level transactional data, and invests significant amounts into consumer research (it is not uncommon for the largest CPG companies to invest hundreds of millions of dollars in primary consumer research). Typically, these companies will use optimization to tackle pricing issues such as promotional pricing, product line pricing, new product pricing, and trade program design.

Historically, optimization has been the bailiwick of industries with perishable inventory, such as hotels, cruise lines, rental-car agencies, and airlines—for example, once a hotel room remains vacant for a night, the revenue for that room on that night is lost forever. Therefore, these industries have developed sophisticated revenue management programs that optimize the price volume tradeoffs for their perishable inventory.

One of the first industries to employ price optimization software was the airline industry. However, even though most airlines have sophisticated optimization models, the majority do not qualify as Level 4 pricers. That is primarily because in many cases, they do not have a solid understanding of customer value. In our language, they have invested in Level 4 before investing in Level 3. The customers of Level 4 pricing organizations think that, even if prices are high, they received good value and, in many cases, have made the decision to pay more to receive additional benefits. These days, our clients often cite Apple as a Level 4 or 5 company. Prices for the latest gadgets may be high, but we line up to pay for them and, in many cases, we willingly pay even more to receive more memory, etc. To be a true Level 4 pricing organization, it is necessary to have differentiated products or services to facilitate the tradeoffs necessary for optimization.

Price optimization is a relatively new discipline in B2B. Even just 10 years ago, these companies rarely applied optimization. Why are they doing so now? The desire has likely always been there, but the main reason price optimization is a goal today is that new technology has put it within reach for most companies.

Two developments in recent years have had a major impact on a company's ability to use optimization.

- The exponential growth in computer power enables organizations to analyze huge amounts of historical sales data and build regression models.
- The invention and maturation of conjoint analysis allows companies to estimate the tradeoff customers make between price and other attributes.

While we are focusing most of this chapter on optimization, a critical challenge at Level 4 is to be able to use statistics and quantitative analysis wisely—that is where the "art" of pricing comes in.

Level 4 optimization must be embedded in a culture of Level 3 wisdom if a company is to achieve a truly lasting competitive advantage. A Level 4 client in the chemical industry, for example, has developed a highly predictive price-optimization model that is very useful for assessing when to change prices. However, it has also developed a Pricing Power Assessment tool that incorporates a number of "softer" measures, such as market conditions and customer sentiment, to evaluate whether or not to adjust prices. Both are important tools to help decide when to adjust prices. Management judgment is a critical element in the decision-making process as well, and it is the combination of these three things that make for great pricing. Hence, the optimization engine is only one piece of the pricing equation. As you can see, Level 4 is about a lot more than pressing a button and getting the answer!

What is Elasticity?

Elasticity is such a seminal concept to Level 4 pricing that we will explain it here to ensure we are all on the same wavelength.

In a nutshell, the demand curve represents the relationship between price and demand, and elasticity is the slope of the demand curve. For example, if price goes up 10% and demand goes down 20%, the product is considered price elastic (-20%/+10% = -2). If, on the other hand, price is raised 10% and demand goes down 5%, the product is price inelastic (-5%/+10% = -0.5). Elasticity of -1.0 is the transition from inelastic to elastic.

The calculation is very simple, but actually determining elasticity is, of course, more difficult. Two of the most common challenges are that elasticity can change with time and circumstance, and that the demand curve (which represents the expected demand at each price in a range) is often not well behaved as we move from one price to the next. We will discuss that in more detail when we describe each of the core methods of estimating elasticity.

Knowledge of elasticity is useful because it enables you to optimize. For example, here are the kinds of questions that elasticity can help answer with precision:

- What is the optimal price for new products?
- Should the price of existing products be increased or decreased?
- What is the optimal price gap between different SKUs/versions within a product line?
- What is the optimal price gap versus a new competitive entrant into the category?
- How can incentives be optimized?
- What is the optimal price structure?
- What is the optimal pricing and program design for channel customers?

The payoff of precision is the ability to maximize the tradeoff between price and volume to achieve sustained improvements in profitability. The simple rule is that if you know the shape of the demand curve and your costs, you can optimize, as demonstrated in *Figure 4.1*.

Figure 4.1

Expected Profit versus Price –
at 2,000 units and $1,550/ton cost

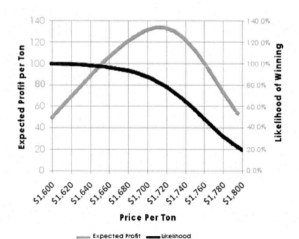

The value of this information is obvious: it allows you to hit the "pricing bull's eye." The improvements in profitability are significant. For example, hotel chain Marriott International recently built a B2B optimization engine for group pricing, and estimates that "the profit improvement . . . in its first two years of use is over $120 million."[3]

One note of caution: The demand curve is not always a smooth line in which demand drops steadily as price increases. In reality, demand curves can be discontinuous, with large cliffs at key price points. In other words, once you price over a "pricing threshold," demand may drop precipitously.

The Culture at Level 4

At Level 4, the pricing manager does not need to be a mathematician who builds sophisticated optimization models. Instead, he or she must become deeply familiar with the various optimization techniques, knowing their strengths and weaknesses for the business, and when to use them.

There are some notable differences between Level 3 and Level 4 companies. Level 4 organizations:

- Make more precise decisions, faster;
- Are open to experimentation with optimization, and consider failure an important learning for future reference;
- Have a high degree of trust—but not blind trust—in optimization;
- Are data driven—they estimate elasticity when and where possible;
- Regularly and consciously make decisions in which they sacrifice volume in favor of profit;
- Are more consistently profitable than their industry peers.

Case study: Global Aviation Manufacturer

Tony was the pricing manager for a $10-billion division of a global multi-national. For the first two years, he spent time putting out fires, gaining control, and mastering the data within the organization. In the subsequent two years, he worked closely with Marketing and Sales in developing a value-based pricing strategy. The effort paid off, and the team delivered hundreds of millions of dollars to the organization after they devised an innovative method of pricing that reduced risk for customers and significantly increased the potential reward for the company. Now Tony was ready to lead the ascent to Level 4. He knew it would be challenging, but he had a plan that he had been crafting for some time now, and he was chomping at the bit to implement it.

First, he assessed the opportunities for optimization. He had attended conferences and read books on price optimization, noting what worked and some of the mistakes other companies had made. He knew that, because his company had a small number of large customers, there would be limited opportunities for using the sales data to run regression models. But there were two places that Tony thought he could profitably apply optimization. The company sold hundreds of thousands of spare parts, and Tony was convinced that price testing could be used to help optimize parts pricing versus the current method of using simple margin-based formulas. The other opportunity was the product development process. Tony noticed that the company often over-specified products, and he thought conjoint research could help the engineering team get closer to the tradeoffs customers made between price and product features.

Tony's two-pronged effort was very profitable. The parts testing project yielded fact-based insight into which parts were highly price-sensitive versus those that were not. But Tony did not rely solely on the data; he also delved deeply into the psychological aspects, and considered how price points fit into the customers' response to price. For example, he found that one spare part had a psychological pricing threshold at $1,000, and exceeding that would lead to customers aggressively shopping elsewhere. These insights *gave management the confidence to raise prices beyond their initial comfort zone on some parts, and helped them realize they should be more conservative with their price on other spare parts.*

Using conjoint analysis in the new product introduction process was Tony's other initiative. The first conjoint analysis study he conducted analyzed the option of developing a Software as a Service (SaaS) offering for customers that allowed them to treat the purchase as an operating expense, versus the existing capital expenditure (CAPEX) solution, which often involved a more stringent approval process. The insights from this research provided tremendous value to the product development team; it enabled them to focus their efforts on the features and attributes for which customers were willing to pay, and to parse out innovation for which customers were not willing to pay much. The result was a streamlined offering that was well designed and priced. The other benefit was that Tony shared the research results with the sales force, which built their confidence so they could execute effectively.

As a result of Tony's successful introduction of optimization to his organization, he has been selected as the go-to person to help all divisions implement optimization. He is also invited to high-level strategy meetings because he brings unique insights and analyses that provide a forward-looking perspective into customer behavior and pricing.

Tony is truly a Level 4 pricer. He has combined the wisdom gained at Level 3 with the precision acquired at Level 4 to create lasting competitive advantage.

Common Objections to Optimization

Price optimization is a relatively new concept, and so there will be some growing pains. Some companies, for example, have tried to use optimization in situations where it really is not appropriate. The result can be frustration and disappointment, as these quotations demonstrate:

- "We bought a pricing software optimization engine, and it did not deliver the results we hoped for."
- "The conjoint results did not make sense. In the end, we went with our gut."
- "We built a regression model with our sales data, but some of the results were illogical. We realized the data was too incomplete to be useful."

One of the key skills is knowing where and when to use optimization. Recently, one client asked us to review his company's attempt at measuring price elasticity. The organization had conducted a very simple analysis that on the surface made perfect sense. It compared last year's prices and sales to this year's, which provided the numbers "needed" to calculate elasticity (change in Q / change in P).

However, the results made no sense. Elasticity ranged from +50 (if you raise price by 1%, demand goes up 50%) to -353 (if you lower price by 1%, demand goes up by 353%). There were two critical deficiencies with the analysis. First, the company did not sell many units of some of its products. For example, it sold five units of one spare part in year one, and 10 units in year two—and increased prices by 2% during that period. The elasticity was calculated to be +50 (+100%/+2% = +50). In fact, all that had happened was that one large customer had a unique need that required it to place a large order for this replacement part. It would not be repeating that order next year, and demand would likely fall back to historical levels.

The second deficiency was that the company's analysis assumed that all of the variation in sales was caused by price changes; its model did not include any insight into other factors, such as technological change, competitive dynamics, or changes in the economy, which can be important drivers of demand. For example, the company had raised prices on one product by 10%, and demand had plummeted from 3,000 units in year one to 1,500 units in year two. A simple elasticity calculation would indicate that the product is highly price-elastic (-50%/+10%

= -5.0). But in fact, this product was becoming obsolete, and lowering price by 10% would not increase demand at all. Instead, a better pricing strategy would have been to milk the product and raise prices for those customers who were unwilling to move to the new technology.

Similar problems may occur with conjoint analysis. We have met with many clients who have been dissatisfied with their results. Conjoint analysis studies are quite tricky to design, and the principle of garbage in/garbage out applies.

But having a bad experience doesn't mean that conjoint cannot be done, or that regression analysis or software optimization engines or testing are not the way to go. There are now many B2B and B2B2C companies that are using optimization successfully, and are gaining advantage over competitors who are not. The key is to take small steps and build confidence. After all, it takes time to embrace change. At Level 4, we are being asked to temporarily set aside our intuitive judgment to consider other possibilities, some of which may seem counter-intuitive.

Case study: Electrical Products Company

An electrical products company was the industry leader in a particular category. It had a well-known brand with the highest market share in its category, and many SKUs as well.

The results of a conjoint study indicated that the product had both the highest loyalty and the highest elasticity. On the surface, these two things seem incompatible because the highest loyalty implies customers will not move due to price, while the highest elasticity implies customers are very price-sensitive. How can these apparently opposing situations exist? The explanation was that the customers did have the highest loyalty to the brand, but they were prepared to change SKUs within the brand based on price. Hence, they were brand loyal, meaning low brand elasticity, but there was high cross-elasticity among SKUs. This finding provided significant insight into how to price more effectively. However, there was real discomfort with the findings until they could be explained in a way that was intuitive (i.e., lead to a deeper understanding of the customer). Therefore, optimization findings ultimately must "make sense."

It is important to realize that people may feel threatened by optimization, particularly if it is replacing or augmenting work that they have previously done. For example, many senior managers, and salespeople as well, view themselves as highly effective pricers, and are therefore reticent to cede control of their pricing decisions to a model.

Here are some pointers to keep in mind as you go through the change management process.

- The first optimization project you do should have a high chance of success. Greater risks can be taken in future projects after you have gotten "some wins" under your belt.
- The socialization of optimization, both the benefits and the limitations, is important in the early stages of going down this road. This way, people will be more patient with obtaining the long-term benefits.
- The sales force, in a sense, has the most to lose, because most optimization projects will price for value, forcing the sales team to sell value rather than discount. Hence, the importance of aligning compensation systems with the goals of the organization. There is no way an organization should adopt a robust price optimization methodology unless a significant portion of compensation is driven by margin.

This quotation from the movie *Moneyball* seems to summarize the potential benefits and the emotional challenges of making the transition to Level 4 in many B2B and B2B2C businesses. But first, a little background. The movie is about Billy Beane, the GM of the Oakland A's major league baseball team, who collaborated with a statistician to achieve unbelievable results. Essentially, they lost four of their top players and used statistical methods to select their replacements, relying less on the judgment and intuitive wisdom of the management team. The management team was displeased, but the results were incredible. In fact, Beane and the statistician achieved one of the greatest turnarounds ever witnessed in professional sports. The quotation below is by the owner of a competing baseball team (Boston Red Sox), who is trying to recruit Beane to his team:

"For $41 million, you built a playoff team. You lost Damon, Giambi, Isringhausen, Pena, and you won more games without them than you did with them. You won the exact same number of games that the Yankees won, but the Yankees spent $1.4 million per win and you paid $260,000. I know you've taken it in the teeth out there, but the first guy through the wall always gets bloody, always. It's the threat of not just the way of doing business, but in their minds it's threatening the game. But really what it's threatening is their livelihoods. It's threatening their jobs; it's threatening the way that they do things. And every time that happens, whether it's the government or a way of doing business or whatever it is . . . they go bat shit crazy. I mean, anybody who's not building a team right and rebuilding it using your model, they're dinosaurs. They'll be sitting on their ass on the sofa in October, watching the Boston Red Sox win the World Series."

Level 4 Processes

Figure 4.2

The Four Core Pricing Processes

In Level 4, companies emphasize the relationships between P1-Setting Pricing Strategy—and P2-Setting Customer Net Prices. Earlier, we commented that airlines were using optimization, but were not true Level 4 pricers. That's because they have focused the optimization on simply setting prices, and have not paid attention to the relationship between the pricing strategy and the impact it should have on the way that prices are offered to customer segments.

In Level 2, companies are concerned with cleaning up the execution of pricing in P3, and spend too much time and attention on costs as a basis for pricing instead of pursuing the more strategic analysis that more sophisticated pricers undertake in P1.

In Level 3, companies spend time understanding value, and how it can change for customers in different segments. Level 3 companies can develop sound value-based pricing strategies that can have a significant impact on the bottom line. So what is the distinction that allows a company to advance to Level 4?

The key difference between Level 3 and Level 4 is the ability of Level 4 organizations to quickly and precisely monetize value. For example, a Level 3 company may know that customers derive double the value moving from the Model 200 to the Model 300 within their product line, but will still be unclear how much of that value they can capture. Should they charge twice as much, 50% more, or some other premium? Level 4 organizations have models they use to guide the decision by optimizing the price gap and resulting changes in demand (mix) and profitability.

In general, there is also a higher level of sophistication in the offer design of Level 4 companies (and this is another possible reason why some firms shy away from Level 4 initiatives). Level 4 companies are more likely to make frequent adjustments to their prices or programs: they may present more alternatives to customers (bundling and unbundling different elements of the offer); or they may make different offers to different segments of customers, using an approach called micro-segmentation.

Level 4 pricing organizations will incorporate one or more of the following changes in their price-setting process to help make the leap from Level 3.

- More frequent price changes. As we explained earlier, elasticity is not constant with time. Level 4 organizations work to forecast these changes (caused by competitive actions, trends, shortages or excesses of supply, etc.). Once they understand the impact the change will have, they may choose to adjust their price.
- Micro-segmentation (more precise segmentation of customers). Many companies have very simple segmentation models using easily obtained data, such as customer size or end-user industry. In Level 4, segmentation must become much more precise. Micro-segmentation is a process in which the company selects five to seven dimensions for segmentation, each of which might have five to ten different

categories or levels. The result is that the customer base is broken into many (frequently more than 1,000) micro-segments. These micro-segments might include customers who look the same in terms of region, order frequency and size, reliance on technical support, loyalty and relationship, product mix or configuration, sales channel, etc. Customer offers are designed to minimize unexplained differences between customers in similar micro-segments.

- Prices and offers are more carefully designed to meet the particular needs of the customer. Since Level 4 companies can understand the tradeoffs they expect customers to make, they can consider a broader range of alternatives and choose the one that optimizes the result. For example, they can offer premium tech support at a high price to customers who place a heavy emphasis on technical support (and who have been determined to have a high willingness to pay for the service). In this offer, perhaps other elements of the offering are scaled back because the customers in this segment don't value them.

- Ultimately, the latitude for people to use their intuition to set the price is reduced in Level 4. This implies that there is going to be a lot of work involved in winning over the sales organization. Simply announcing the elimination of all negotiation will ensure that Sales will actively resist your initiative. Salespeople must be given the opportunity to gain confidence in the new pricing model, and must also be shown ways that they can still manage the account. You want to give them more ways to deliver offers that customers value, and the confidence to know that if they sell the value, customers will pay the asking price. We should point out that, despite the presence of a highly precise optimization engine, the sales department has a role to play. Negotiation ranges can be reduced, but cannot be eliminated.

Scenario Planning (Assess Viability)

One of the main changes in the progression to Level 4 is the need to assess multiple options as you implement your strategy. A price optimization tool will enable this process, but in many cases it is driven by the creativity of the pricing team. In this process, the business leaders generate a number of potential approaches to achieve the goals. Some optimization engines can consider all possible alternatives and spit out the single optimal answer, but often, pricing decisions are more nuanced than that.

Having a well-developed scenario planning process ensures the organization is comfortable generating alternatives, modeling the impact, assessing the outcome, and selecting a result. Often, companies will focus their optimization efforts solely on the ability of an alternative to generate the best bottom line. Experienced Level 4 companies remember the lessons they learned in Level 3 about value. They will therefore look carefully at the impact of their actions on their current and prospective customers. Which customers stand to win (or lose) if we implement the change in this manner? Is that acceptable? Are there longer-term impacts that might result that are not considered in our optimization engine?

The concept of optimizing pricing decisions based on long-term impacts is an important one. Price optimization has been the subject of many articles in recent years. Most of those articles have concluded that, to optimize prices, you should figure out the demand curve, link it to the cost function, and find the point where marginal revenue equals marginal costs. While this might provide the answer from an economic point of view, it doesn't measure up from the standpoint of a Level 4 approach. That's because it yields a short-term optimization that doesn't account for the longer-term impact on customers, or for potential competitive reactions.

Many companies have built a stable core of customers who represent a stream of future revenues and profits. Customer

Lifetime Value (CLV) models seek to model the future cash flows for each customer segment. The underlying concept is not difficult to understand: today's customers will make purchases and generate revenues and (hopefully) profits in the future; estimating future purchases and valuing them in today's dollars is the CLV. The objective in a CLV model is to maximize the Net Present Value (NPV) of these expected future cash flows. The analysis becomes more difficult as we think about all the potential futures we could have with each segment of customers:

1. The relationship could deepen, and customers will buy our offerings at an increased rate.
2. The relationship could sour, or we could become less relevant to the customer in the future, and our business with them will shrink.
3. We may not really have a relationship with this segment of customers at all, and they may dip in and out of our business, and "churn" through our system.

The possibilities are endless, and the intent here is not to detail the steps for creating a model for CLV. Rather, we want to look at the impact of pricing on the possible future outcomes, and discuss how the "Price/Volume/Profit Tool," a vital element for achieving Level 4 of the World-Class Pricing framework, links to this model.

Businesses typically have two basic objectives: to maximize profit and growth. These are often expressed as one unified goal: profitable growth. But more often than not, one of these objectives is achieved at the expense of the other, rather than both simultaneously.

If we were to plot these objectives on a graph, with Customer Growth on the "x" axis and Profit Growth on the "y" axis, it would look like *Figure 4.3*. The business would follow some trajectory within the box (shown as the arrows inside).

Figure 4.3

Profit Growth versus Customer Growth

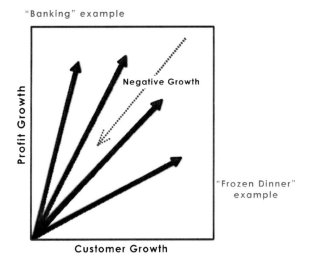

"Banking" example

Profit Growth

Negative Growth

"Frozen Dinner" example

Customer Growth

But let's think of those arrows in terms of the available strategies. We had a client recently—a bank—that was trying to maximize the profit from the cash customers would invest in its savings-account product. The simplest way to do this would be to cut the savings rate paid to customers. The bank had a large book of business, and history showed that customers were slow to react by pulling their money out of the savings instrument. Therefore, this would all but guarantee at least two very profitable years, as the bank would save a considerable amount of interest expense on its entire book of business. But what would happen in the future? Even though the profit forecast did not immediately show it, it was clear that the business would suffer, and ultimately, so would long-term profitability. In terms of our model, the initial move is up the "y" axis, but you can envision the path turning left and heading down over time.

In another example, in the frozen-dinner category, we see a very different path. This category, sold through grocery retailers, is heavily promoted. Customers had been trained to wait to buy at a discounted price. They would enter the category to buy a product on promotion, but in general, showed little loyalty to specific brands. What was worse, these promotions were only marginally profitable, and required extensive resources to manage them effectively. Looking at our model, the promotions had a large impact on customer growth (providing some justification to continue this course), but only a slight positive impact on profit. They showed limited ability to move customers solidly into the franchise so that they could be counted on to deliver future profitable (full price) sales. In effect, this was a move almost straight along the horizontal axis. Eventually, even loyal customers would catch on and become "system beaters" (customers who figure out how to beat the system), and long-term profitability would begin to fall.

In both cases, a pricing decision had an important impact on the business's trajectory in *Figure 4.3*. The question is: which strategy should the pricing manager pursue?

Our belief is the effectiveness of a pricing strategy has to be measured over the long term, and not solely by its ability to deliver quarterly, or even annual, profit and growth targets.

Your business has an available margin pool (the total available margin that customers are prepared to generate in a given segment over the product life cycle). The objective of the pricing strategy is to capture as much of that margin pool as possible. A number of factors might affect that result.

1. A price increase—harvests the value from existing customers, but if not supported by a corresponding improvement in customer value (perceived or financial), the active customer base will shrink, and the NPV of future cash flows may erode. The exceptions are markets experiencing rapid growth, or inflationary markets.
2. Deals and promotions—bring new customers into the franchise, and encourage existing customers to buy more. They provide the potential for growth

(usually with price-sensitive customers), but if these lower-priced purchasers cannot be fenced off from the full-price-paying customers, or can't increase the base of profitable customers, profitability will erode.

3. Change pricing structure (e.g., bundles, solutions pricing, price fences, tiered offerings, etc.)—can drive deeper, broader relationships with existing customers and draw new, profitable customers into the margin pool.

Pricing management plays a critical role in the business's trajectory into the future. The model presents three basic strategic paths for the pricing manager to follow. Our experience shows that effective pricing managers will choose strategies that involve each of the three major trajectories: price optimization of the everyday business through price increases or decreases; optimization of promotions for growth and profit; and changes to the pricing structure.

As part of a strategic approach to price increases (or decreases), pricing managers often invest in research to develop an understanding of price elasticity, including the cross-elasticity of products in the portfolio (more about that later). Even without changes to the pricing structure, this information enables them to optimize profit and expected volume.

In the case of promotions, the optimization has to consider both the tangible and intangible effects. The pricing manager can analyze transactional data to understand the expected lift and profit, as well as the "stickiness" with customers. Taking a more strategic viewpoint leads the pricing manager to think about potential competitive reaction and customer expectations that deals are always going to be available.

Ultimately, the optimization of both everyday prices and promotions leads pricing managers to focus on segmentation. More effective segmentation, as well as a pricing structure that responds to the needs of specific segments, provides an opportunity to improve both growth and profit in the long term—the "Holy Grail" of pricing. *Figure 4.4* shows the strategic alternatives (a section on price structure with a case study is provided later in this chapter under Level 4 Strategies).

Figure 4.4

Pricing's Strategic Alternatives

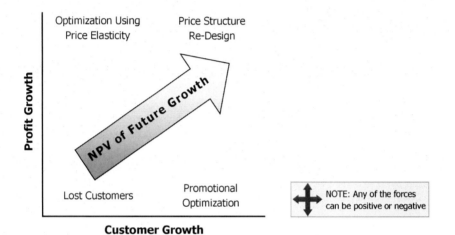

Optimization Tools

There are three core tools that companies can use for price optimization:

- Conjoint analysis (survey methodology);
- Transactional analysis;
- Testing.

Each method has its strengths and weaknesses. In *Table 4.1*, we have summarized the relative areas of strength and weakness. In the rest of the section, we will discuss these in more detail, and provide case studies of each method.

Table 4.1

Optimization Tools

Pricing Issue	Testing	Discrete Choice	Regression
New Product	●	●	○
Price Increase/ Decrease	●	●	◗
Product Line Optimization	○	●	●
Impulse Items	●	◗	◗
New Competitor	◗	●	◗
Promotional Optimization	●	○	●
Price Structure	○	●	○
Price Segmentation	○	●	○
Channel Growth	◗	○	○

Excellent ●   Good ◗   Poor ○

Conjoint Research

The word "conjoint" means "consider jointly." It is a powerful method, and has evolved greatly over the past 30 years.

Conjoint essentially involves presenting customers with scenarios in which they must compare and contrast alternative offers, and either indicate their preferences or make choices among them. There are many different variations of conjoint research, including: Full Profile Conjoint, Max/Diff, Adaptive Conjoint Analysis, Discrete Choice (also known as Choice-Based Conjoint or CBC), Menu-Based Conjoint (MBC), or Adaptive

Choice-Based Conjoint (ACBC). But it is the choice-based methods (CBC, ACBC) that are most suitable for pricing.

Preference-based conjoint involves some type of scoring or ranking (e.g., rank your preferences from "most likely to purchase" to "least likely to purchase"), whereas choice-based is selecting a particular option versus other options.

A well-designed Discrete Choice conjoint study feels very realistic to the respondent because it does a good job of mimicking the actual buying process that customers go through. That is what makes Discrete Choice so powerful. By making tradeoffs between price and product/service attributes, we can estimate the utility of each attribute. We can then determine how much people are willing to pay, and the optimal price and product configuration versus the competition. A case study is provided later to demonstrate this powerful pricing tool.

Adaptive Choice-Based Conjoint (ACBC) is very similar to Discrete Choice in that it uses the same principles to get at the utilities of the product/service benefits. The key difference is that ACBC can handle many more attributes. Whereas Discrete Choice can handle 4-7 attributes and their sub-levels (an example of an attribute is price, and the sub-levels are the different price points tested), ACBC offers the possibility of testing 30-50 attributes. Most companies do not require this level of detail; in fact, if they do, it may be because they have not thought through the customers' point of view (customers simplify, and rarely consider more than 4-7 factors when they make a buying decision). But there are industries that have complex product offers, and customers have to make tradeoffs among many different attributes. ACBC is invaluable for these situations.

Of the more than 700 price optimization studies Pricing Solutions has executed, approximately 90% of them utilize Discrete Choice. Therefore, we will concentrate our efforts in this section on that method.

Discrete Choice has been used in virtually every industry, and has proven over time to be a reliable predictor of price elasticity. The reason it is considered the gold standard is that it best replicates the real-life buying process that customers go through by forcing them to select one option.

Discrete Choice can be used to optimize many pricing decisions, including new product pricing, product line pricing (e.g., gaps between SKUs), trade channel programs, price structure (e.g., rebates, warranties, volume discounts, etc.), product configuration, price segmentation, and price setting for existing products.

The most common of the above pricing issues for which Discrete Choice is used is new product pricing. New products are a vital source of growth and future profits. Companies don't want to leave money on the table, nor do they want to threaten the success of the launch by pricing too high. Discrete Choice is a very powerful way of obtaining insight into the optimal pricing strategy. We find that most clients end up pricing higher than they had initially planned once they have done a Discrete Choice study because they are much more confident about the value of their new products, and now have the facts needed to build the confidence of the sales force. They are also much clearer on who is in their core market and with whom they should not plan on doing business.

Case study: Animal Health Pharmaceutical Product

A company specializing in pharmaceuticals for livestock developed a new product that had several important advantages: it helped reduce the mortality rate of sick animals; it had a shorter duration of therapy; the animals required fewer injections; and less milk was discarded. The critical question facing the team was how to price the new product. They knew they wanted to be premium priced, but by how much? What was the tradeoff between price and volume? The company conducted an online Discrete Choice study with milk producers (e.g., farmers) and veterinarians. Figure 4.5 shows an example of a scenario in which the respondents were asked to choose one of three options. They were typically asked to make 10 to 12 choices. Each time they did so, they were essentially indicating how they traded off price versus the other attributes. The results of their choices could be used to estimate the utility of each attribute and the amount the customer was willing to pay.

Figure 4.5

Discrete Choice Scenario

Research Methodology—Online Survey
Discrete Choice Scenarios

Scenario 1 of 12
Please review and select which product best meets your needs for your **1st line hospital BRD treatment program** for cattle that have **NOT been mass treated.**

ATTRIBUTES	Product A	Product B	Product C
Overall Reduction in Morbidity/Mortality/Repulls	Industry Standard	Above Standard	Industry Standard
Labeled Pathogens	P. Haemolytica + P Multocida + H Somnus	P. Haemolytica + P Multocida + H Somnus + Footrot	P. Haemolytica + P Multocida
Duration of Antibiotic Therapy in a Single Injection	4 days	3 days	> 7 days
Number of Injections per Treatment Regimen	Multiple injections	Multiple injections	Single injection
Pre-Slaughter Withdrawal	2-4 days	23-28 days	0 days
Price per 500lb Dose with Disease Event	$10.50	$14.50	$12.50

Please click on the one product you would likely use: ○ ○ ○

The results of this exercise were used to construct the shares of Client and the competitive products at different price levels.

The survey data is used to construct a predictive pricing model that estimates revenue, market share, and margins. The results of this study led to the development of a model similar to *Figure 4.6*.

Figure 4.6
Discrete Choice Scenarios - Pricing Model

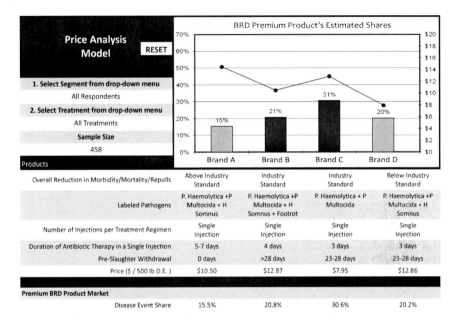

Products		Brand A	Brand B	Brand C	Brand D
Overall Reduction in Morbidity/Mortality/Repulls		Above Industry Standard	Industry Standard	Industry Standard	Below Industry Standard
Labeled Pathogens		P. Haemolytica +P Multocida + H Somnus	P. Haemolytica +P Multocida + H Somnus + Footrot	P. Haemolytica + P Multocida	P. Haemolytica +P Multocida + H Somnus
Number of Injections per Treatment Regimen		Single Injection	Single Injection	Single Injection	Single Injection
Duration of Antibiotic Therapy in a Single Injection		5-7 days	4 days	3 days	3 days
Pre-Slaughter Withdrawal		0 days	>28 days	23-28 days	23-28 days
Price ($ / 500 lb D.E.)		$10.50	$12.87	$7.95	$12.86
Premium BRD Product Market					
Disease Event Share		15.5%	20.8%	30.6%	20.2%

The model enables the user to select the customer segment (e.g., veterinarians, large beef producers, small beef producers, etc.) and to vary the pricing, not only of the new product, but of all existing competitive offers as well. This enables the company to estimate profitability, revenue, and market share at different price levels, as demonstrated in *Figure 4.7*.

Figure 4.7

Profit Optimization Forecast

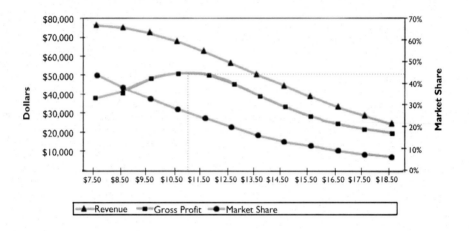

In this particular case, the client thought that if it chose the "optimal" price of $11.00, its market share would be close to 45%. That would cause its competitors to react by lowering their prices to protect their market share.

To assess the risk of competitive response, the client ran different scenarios based on management judgment. *Figure 4.8* shows a critical insight obtained from the output of those changes. Based on the assumptions about competitive response, the revised optimal price is, in fact, $13.00. At this level, senior management was confident that the competition would not react by lowering prices.

Figure 4.8

Optimal Price Given Competitive Assumptions

Scenario 1
• Optimal price is
  $11.00, assuming no
  competitve response

Scenario 2
• Revised forecast
  based on expected
  competitive response.
  Optimal price is now
  $13.00

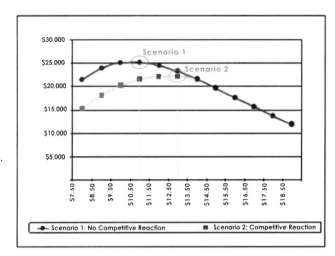

In the end, it turned out that the senior management team was correct. With our client's product priced at $13.00, the competition did not lower price. This was very beneficial because, instead of getting into a price war, our client led the category with a price increase the following year, and the competition followed suit.

Juxtapose this with the case of another pharmaceutical company that had not done the necessary homework to understand the value of its product, and instead priced low to rapidly grow market share. One year after the launch of an important new drug, a price war started and the company estimated that it had left $500 million on the table.

Following are some important things to keep in mind about conducting a Discrete Choice pricing study.

1. Most studies today are conducted via the Web, because you can build logic into the survey, customized for each respondent. For example, the respondent can be asked

questions that customize scenarios based on his or her awareness of competing alternatives. This level of customization leads to deeper insights and better overall predictiveness. You can also provide effective video demonstrations of new products, so customers more fully appreciate each product's value. And it is less expensive to execute because of the relative ease of accessing a sample.

2. If you have a market research department, it is helpful to engage them in this process. However, many B2B companies do not have large research departments, so you may have to lead this as your own initiative.

3. An alternative is doing conjoint studies on your own. For example, a software system called Sawtooth can be used to do pricing research. The disadvantage of this method, however, is that pricing research is one of the most difficult to conduct accurately. It requires expertise to design and execute it properly. Most companies will not have the resources or the volume of studies needed to develop that expertise.

Testing

Testing involves doing a pricing experiment in the marketplace. It is commonly used in direct mail and is increasingly being used on the Web, but in both situations the focus is typically B2C.

However, testing is also occasionally used in the B2B context. For example, it works quite well in parts pricing (you will recall Tony, the pricing manager for a global multinational, who executed a parts pricing test), promotions, and changes in price structure.

Case study: Pricing Structure Test in Financial Services

A transaction processing company (which processes debit and credit for retailers) was replacing paper statements with electronic ones. Even though sending statements electronically would reduce costs, the v.p. marketing, a good value-based pricer, perceived that it also increased value and could be an opportunity to capture price.

To assess the situation, the company conducted a test with a random sample of 1,500 customers out of its total base of 60,000 businesses. It broke the sample into three cells. Customers in each cell received a letter announcing the new service and describing its many benefits, such as 24/7 access to statements. The only difference was that Cell A customers would be charged an incremental fee of $1 per month; Cell B customers would be charged $2 per month; and Cell C customers would receive the introductory service free of charge. The company used the number of complaints received as the metric to assess the impact of the different pricing strategies.

The difference in the number of complaints registered for each cell was both minimal and statistically insignificant. As a result of these findings, the company had the confidence to implement a $2-per-month charge for the electronic statement. That strategy has contributed more than $10 million annually to the bottom line. Had the company not conducted the test, it never would have had the confidence to execute such a bold pricing strategy. A very profitable test indeed!

Case study: Promotional Price Tests in the Airline Industry

Price tests can be a great way to assess the impact of different promotions.

A leading global airline regularly runs promotional tests. For example, the company wanted to grow market share for key high-traffic routes, and perceived an opportunity to do so with business travelers. Business travel is often booked mere days in advance, and the cost of a ticket for a short-haul flight can easily be three to four times more than a fare booked two weeks in advance. This annoys business customers, as the price variation between what they paid and what they would have paid two weeks prior can be a factor of 200 to 300%.

From the airline's perspective, it hurts the relationship with those customers and encourages them to shop aggressively for a better price.

To find some middle ground, the airline launched a test in which it sold books of flight passes at reduced rates for high-traffic routes. The goal was to secure market share and a reasonable average price, while giving customers the opportunity to avoid paying exorbitant prices when they have a short booking window.

The test was a success, and this pricing structure has now become a part of the overall offering.

Case study: Chocolate Bars

One very successful project that we conducted involved a price test in the chocolate bar category. Many years ago, the product category in this particular region was locked in a horrific price war. While the price of a regular 50-gram bar had risen to $0.79, there seemed to be a powerful magnet drawing the companies to promote at the 2-for-$0.99 price point. Even though they were losing money on the second bar, the volume lift was significant and difficult to resist.

When we met with the company, we started with the corporate office. They felt the solution would be to reduce the size of the bar from 50g to 37g and continue to promote at 2 for $0.99. We convinced them to let the data lead us to a solution. (Side note: we did see one confectionery company so locked on the $0.99 price point that it held the price for 35 years, reducing the product from 150g to 25g over that time.)

In this case, with a highly impulse-driven category, research would never work. "How many chocolate bars would you buy at 2 for

$0.99?" Response: "I am not sure. How hot is it? Am I hungry? How many of my children are in the car?" We designed and implemented a price test in which we took over the pricing and promotions of all chocolate bars in the category at a statistically significant number of convenience stores for a period of 12 weeks.

The results were clear. We created an index of demand, with the value of 100 representing the demand for a single-bar price at an everyday price of $0.79. Demand spiked when we promoted at 2 for $0.99, hitting an index of 300. Demand dropped markedly when the price crossed the dollar threshold to 2 for $1.09 with an index of 130, but it held constant at 130 when we promoted at 2 for $1.09 and 2 for $1.29. The demand curve was clearly not the nice smooth curve you see in textbooks.

Figure 4.9

Chocolate Bar Demand Curve

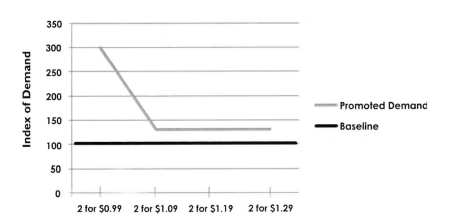

The situation became even more compelling when we interviewed the factory manager. We had been told that the plant was capacity-limited. When we asked where the bottleneck lay, he replied that it was in the packaging line, and that due to space constraints, it would be extremely expensive to alleviate the problem. Reducing the

size of the bars would have actually reduced the available tonnage! Thinking creatively about the problem, the team determined that introducing a new 75g King Size bar would enable us to still have an offering that could be promoted at the important $0.99 price point and increase the tonnage output from the plant. Implementation was a challenge, as it involved redesigning the offer to the trade customers as well. It also meant convincing salespeople to persuade their buyers to try the new offer. But ultimately, it led to a significant improvement in profitability.

If you are going to do testing, it's important that you approach it like a scientific experiment. Many companies have run tests only to find out that they were not rigorous enough to pass the internal data-killing objections from the team. We have seen many organizations try testing, only to throw out the results. To avoid this situation, we have listed some common objections, along with suggestions on how to handle them.

Table 4.2

Objection/Response

Objection	Response
Sample is too small.	Need statistically significant sample. This implies you must have a large enough customer base to drive statistically significant results. Also be sure to consider segmentation in your design.
Changes in market render results useless.	Include impact of market changes in analysis of results, utilizing a control group to establish a baseline.
Test was unrealistic.	Design test with input from all relevant parties (particularly sales force and senior management).
Competitors made changes during time of test.	Include impact of competitive change in analysis of the control and test groups.
Duration of test was too short to know if this reflects long-term behaviour.	Ensure test is of sufficient duration to reflect decisions made by informed customers.
Test set in motion a series of competitive responses that ultimately made it impossible to stop the test at the end of the testing time period.	Consider expected competitive response, or choose a test area so small as to not impact profitability if the test cannot be taken back out of the market.

Figure 4.10 shows a six-step process that should be used to design and execute a test that will be accepted within the organization. In this process, we apply the rigor of a Six Sigma Design of Experiments methodology.

Figure 4.10

Price Testing Process

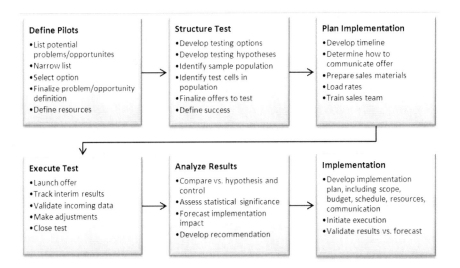

Transactional Analysis

As mentioned at the start of the chapter, one of the most common approaches to optimization and achievement of Level 4 is the analysis of transactional data. The path has been blazed by B2C companies with perishable inventory (such as airlines and hotels). Developers of products and apps sold online are also moving quickly in this area, and are trying to formulate approaches that allow them to adjust their prices in response to changes in demand. The key enabler of transactional optimization is a good forecast of demand as a function of price and other variables. Many B2B companies oversimplify the problem and assume that price is the primary driver of demand. They have expensive sales forces and elaborate account management practices, but all that is meaningless in an oversimplified transaction model.

There are several approaches to optimization using transaction analysis, including the optimization of the product offering/ configuration ladder, price/volume optimization, and micro-segmentation. Earlier in the chapter, we discussed the tradeoffs customers make in selecting the configuration of their offering, and we will review micro-segmentation later. So let's focus here on price/volume optimization using transactional data.

The first question to address is: what data is required to perform transaction optimization? In a B2B setting, it is not sufficient to perform price/volume optimization using win-only data. Consider *Table 4.3.*

Table 4.3

Transaction Optimization Data

Price = % of List Price	Volume	Revenue	Volume (Cumulative)	Revenue (Cumulative)
100%	1	$120	1	$120
98%	117	$14,040	118	$14,160
96%	144	$17,280	262	$31,440
94%	153	$18,360	415	$49,800
92%	226	$27,120	641	$76,920
90%	368	$44,160	1009	$121,080
88%	147	$17,640	1156	$138,720
86%	58	$6,960	1214	$145,680
84%	147	$17,640	1361	$163,320
82%	232	$27,840	1593	$191,160
80%	463	$55,560	2056	$246,720

If we plot price versus volume, we generate what looks like a very well-behaved demand curve. It is downward sloping, and has a nice s-curve shape that is often used in demand models.

Figure 4.11

Price versus Volume

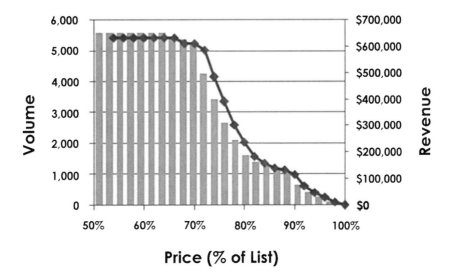

Price (% of List)

However, the problem is that the data represents only what the customer actually paid; it does not include customers who chose not to do business with the company, and, more importantly, it does not indicate what the customer would have been willing to pay if only the salesperson had made the offer at that price. A case in point: we had a client some years ago who did a beautiful job creating a financial value model for its machine tools, but at the end of the presentation, the company had captured none of the value it had identified. Its customers paid a range of prices, and, plotted against volume, the chart would have been similar in shape to the one above. However, the slope did *not* represent elasticity, but rather, only what the salesperson had chosen to offer.

The data that will dramatically improve the accuracy of a transaction optimization model relates to lost deals. Collecting data on lost deals in a B2B context is not simple. A lost deal never enters the transaction system, since there is no transaction *per se*. It requires some finesse to develop a definition of a lost deal to which the organization agrees and for which data is available. Often, the offer is made one month, but the customer doesn't take delivery for several months. It may also be the case that a customer never really fully declines your offer. How do you distinguish between a deal that is pending and a deal that is truly lost? This challenge is not insurmountable, but it does require some work up front to establish the rules and norms.

To improve the quality of the model, you should determine which variables you have access to that might impact the likelihood of winning or losing a deal. In a B2B context, companies have many strategies for increasing switching costs, and these must be considered. For example, one model we built for a company providing business supplies contained the following:

- Quoted price;
- Potential volume;
- Competitive price pressure; competitive pricing;
- Customer relationship strength/incumbency (which could be a simple 1 to 5 scale);
- Sole supplier versus a supplier;
- Estimated switching cost;
- Customer behavioral segments;
- Bundle or product configuration.

A good CRM package will help to organize all the data. Judging by the list above, you will need to enlist the buy-in and support from Sales. But remember, they aren't paid to feed optimization models; keep your request simple and use your system to populate what you can. This is another reason we emphasize the need to complete Level 3 (Partner) before moving to Level 4.

Even when all the data has been compiled, the challenges are not behind us. The shape of the demand curve is non-linear. And yet, if we think of it as smooth, without the cliffs so prevalent in B2C settings, there will still be customers who are very loyal, customers who make tradeoffs, and customers who are not interested. This creates an s-shaped demand curve, and to model this, we need to utilize logistic regression rather than linear regression. Although the concept of logistic regression is straightforward enough—we are trying to create a best fit line—the math is significantly more complicated, and beyond the scope of this book. The output of the model is a curve that shows the likelihood of winning a given deal (somewhere between 0% and 100%) as a function of price and the other variables above.

The output could look something like *Table 4.4* (disguised output from the business supplies company).

Table 4.4

Input	
Customer segment	A
Product code	002245
List price	$150.^{00}
Unit cost	$36.^{00}
Deal volume	150 units
Quote (% of list)	52%

Output	
Estimated win %	91%
Estimated profit (unit profit X volume X win %)	$5,733

Optimization	
Optimal quote (% of list)	85%
Estimated win %	68%
Estimated profit (unit profit X volume X win %)	$9,301

Notice that the expected profit opportunity using the optimization engine (considering win %) is about 60% more than the expected profit without it ($9,301 versus $5,733—see *Tables 4.5 and 4.6*). The upside is significant. However, the likelihood of winning is significantly lower. This approach may hit some hurdles along the way. It may require a lot of coaching for the sales team to accept the strategy of focusing on fewer, yet higher-profit opportunities, especially if the volume of deals is low and it impacts their personal success. For example, if each salesperson has only one customer, he or she will not support a recommended deal price that predicts only a 68% chance of winning.

The model allows us to plan a number of alternative scenarios, and by running it a number of times, we can complete *Table 4.5.*

Table 4.5

Estimated Win %

Volume	Price (% of list)						
	100%	95%	90%	85%	80%	75%	70%
5	71%	76%	80%	83%	86%	89%	91%
15	70%	75%	79%	83%	86%	88%	91%
25	69%	73%	78%	82%	85%	88%	90%
50	65%	70%	75%	79%	83%	86%	89%
75	62%	67%	72%	77%	81%	84%	87%
100	58%	64%	69%	74%	78%	82%	85%
125	54%	60%	66%	71%	76%	80%	83%
150	51%	57%	62%	68%	73%	77%	81%
200	43%	49%	55%	61%	66%	71%	76%
300	30%	35%	40%	46%	52%	58%	64%
400	19%	23%	27%	32%	37%	43%	49%
500	11%	14%	17%	20%	25%	29%	34%

Table 4.6

Expected Profit –
Estimated Win% x Profit/Unit x Volume

		Price (% of list)						
		100%	95%	90%	85%	80%	75%	70%
Volume	5	$405.10	$403.20	$395.10	$381.50	$363.00	$340.40	$314.30
	15	$1,194	$1,192	$1,171	$1,133	$1,080	$1,014	$938
	25	$1,954	$1,955	$1,926	$1,868	$1,784	$1,678	$1,554
	50	$3,718	$3,749	$3,718	$3,628	$3,483	$3,291	$3,059
	75	$5,280	$5,367	$5,362	$5,265	$5,084	$4,828	$4,506
	100	$6,629	$6,795	$6,841	$6,766	$6,574	$6,276	$5,885
	125	$7,761	$8,024	$8,144	$8,115	$7,938	$7,623	$7,185
	150	$8,674	$9,047	$9,261	$9,301	$9,164	$8,857	$8,395
	200	$9,864	$10,474	$10,911	$11,144	$11,154	$10,937	$10,499
	300	$10,090	$11,081	$11,954	$12,649	$13,110	$13,290	$13,160
	400	$8,517	$9,613	$10,689	$11,686	$12,535	$13,164	$13,503
	500	$6,381	$7,342	$8,349	$9,366	$10,340	$11,206	$11,887

The shaded boxes show the optimal price for each volume. *Figure 4.12* shows it graphically.

Figure 4.12

Profit Optimization: 150-Unit Order

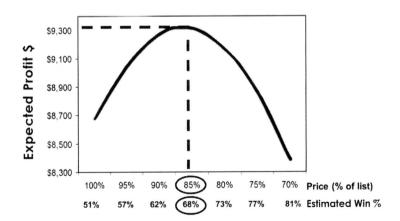

This was a simplified example that neglected the other optimization variables we listed above, but the point is that having a forecast model allows you to consider different ways to approach an opportunity with a customer. There is a tendency for Sales to tell us that "each customer is unique." While that is true if you are bidding on a contract to build a hydroelectric dam, there are many opportunities to apply the concept of optimization in a B2B context. The best way to overcome the trap that each customer is unique is by finding patterns and building models.

Micro-Segmentation

We defined micro-segmentation earlier in this chapter as one of the key processes for Level 4. While theoretically, micro-segmentation is an optimization technique, in practical application, it often does not contain any optimization code. We explained previously that in conducting a micro-segmentation exercise, a company selects five to seven dimensions on which to segment customers that, when combined, can create several hundred (or more) micro-segments. Theoretically, it is possible to estimate the demand curve based on transaction data in each segment. However, in practical terms, this is win-only data in a B2B environment—a situation that, as we explained, is not conducive to price optimization.

But even without running an "optimization engine," we gladly accept micro-segmentation as an optimization technique in B2B environments where there are thousands of customers and transactions. Consider, for example, the following case.

Case study: A Profusion of Parts

Steve managed a parts business in which several thousand customers completed 120,000 or more transactions per year. The business comprised about 5,000 active parts of which fewer than 800 were the biggest sellers. Steve had worked hard to gain the trust of the sales team and bring the pricing process under control. Level 3 was more of a challenge in this business where loyalty was low and it was easy to switch suppliers.

However, as we worked with Steve in Level 3, some important variables began to emerge. We found differences in customer behavior by region and end-user industry that Sales could attribute to competitive intensity, historical development, and the way in which the parts were used. In Level 3, we identified the high-volume products with less differentiation, the specialty products, and the last-minute order builders that no one paid much attention to because they were the last thing anyone thought about when placing an order (and one of the best opportunities to capture margin).

As described above, we have just identified about 50 segments based on six regions multiplied by three end-user industry groups times three product types (remember that not all intersections will have a relevant amount of data). With only 50 segments, it is possible to develop a margin strategy and target for each, and the "optimization process" becomes relatively simple—bring each deal up to the margin target. If we expanded our micro-segmentation model to 500 segments, developing a strategy for each is likely no longer possible. However, it is possible to review each proposed deal against a relevant set of comparable deals. Now you have a valid context against which to evaluate the deal. Simply moving each deal towards the average will result in prices that, while not really "optimized," are the outcome of a process we consider to be Level 4.

Level 4 Strategies

Level 4 pricing is more about precision than strategy. The strategies that have been developed at Level 3 are often retained at Level 4, but are applied more precisely. The key enhancement is that at Level 4, the strategy is executed in such a way that the pricing bull's eye is hit more frequently.

Price optimization can be applied in many areas of pricing strategy, but the improvement is most noticeable in these three:

- New product pricing;
- Channel price optimization;
- Price structure.

In the case studies that follow, we demonstrate some of the pricing strategy decisions that are enhanced by optimization.

New Product Pricing

The pricing of new products is arguably one of the most important decisions a company can make, as new products significantly impact future revenues. Overpricing results in too few sales, while underpricing leads to leaving money on the table.

There is much evidence that companies tend to underprice innovation because they lack confidence in their value proposition. In fact, one leading global company estimated that it left hundreds of millions of dollars on the table over several years because of underpricing new product innovations relative to their value.

Level 4 pricing can dramatically increase a company's confidence in its ability to capture a premium price. Choice-based conjoint (CBC) is the optimization method typically used for new product pricing, as it offers many benefits:

- Improved forecasting at different prices;
- Deeper insight into customer segmentation;
- Detailed insight into the value of the various attributes of the product;
- Improved understanding of the tradeoffs made versus competitive offers.

Case study: Building Systems

A global company in the building systems business was undergoing a transformation in its core business. Historically, it had sold capital equipment, but was in the process of moving to a SaaS-based business model.

The business was complex, as it had many different customer segments and regions with varying needs.

With the new SaaS-based offer in development, the company needed answers to the following foundational questions:

- *How receptive are customers to the SaaS model?*
- *Does it vary by segment?*
- *Who would be the decision-makers? Do they value the solution differently?*
- *What attributes are customers willing to pay for?*
- *How much would they pay?*
- *What price structure should be used to optimize price and market share?*

To answer those questions, the company undertook extensive research. That yielded powerful insights that the organization applied to develop its pricing strategy.

It set a price structure and level, developed customer segmentation, and shared the research with the sales force to ensure they would buy into the strategy. As a result of gaining deep customer understanding, the company launched a premium-priced SaaS offering that has been very well received by customers.

Channel Price Optimization

Selling through distribution channels is a significant pricing challenge that many companies face. When you sell through a channel, you essentially lose control of your pricing to the end user. The key, therefore, is to successfully influence the channel to execute the desired price to the end user. Optimization can play an important role in achieving that goal.

Case study: Office Products

An office products manufacturer sold through distribution. The end users of its products were businesses.

The company sold a product that was the gold standard of its category and enabled it to charge a significant premium. However, recently, distributors were pushing back on price, saying their business customers were not willing to pay the premium price and that new lower priced alternatives were becoming more attractive. The president firmly believed that businesses would pay the premium because of the products' performance advantages but his opinion was not going to sway distributors, he was going to have to prove it.

Therefore, the company conducted a choice-based conjoint (CBC) study to understand the tradeoffs businesses made between price, performance and brand. The results indicated that 80% of businesses were very performance focused and relatively price insensitive—they would pay the price!

But about 20% of businesses were price sensitive, and they were the ones complaining to the distributors about price and threatening to switch. The sales team received coaching, and then shared this research with their distributors. The message was clear: "We are not trying to be all things to all people; we are satisfied with our pricing being appealing to 80% of the market, and do not want to lower our price to do business with the other 20%."

Still, to protect its premium brand, the company launched a lower-priced product under a different brand name. Distributors understood and agreed with the strategy. As a result, the company was able to protect its premium price. Ten years later, it is still charging a premium. The estimated value of successfully influencing the channel over those 10 years is a whopping $300-million incremental margin.

Price Structure

Optimization can significantly enhance price structure by providing a deeper understanding of the tradeoffs that customers make, and segmentation.

A good price structure has several benefits:

- Ensures that price is linked to value delivered;
- Links price to cost to serve, to ensure all customers are profitable;
- Increases revenue by leveraging bundling and other opportunities to enhance value;
- Is intuitive to customers, so they feel they are receiving value as they pay price;
- Enables a company to sell to more segments of the market profitably;
- Enhances sales force execution because the price structure is intuitive.

Case study: Global Financial Services

The corporate banking division of a global financial services company was experiencing increased price sensitivity from its global banking customers, and was unsure whether to cut services in an effort to lower prices and protect market share.

The company invested in a discrete-choice study that provided customers with tradeoffs between different service levels and prices. The results showed there were two segments of customers: highly price sensitive and highly service sensitive. The study also furnished rich insight into the service delivery capabilities for which customers were willing to pay.

Based on these findings, the bank built a three-tiered offering. One option was very price-competitive but included a basic level of service. For the service-sensitive segment, the company provided a bundled offering that included high levels of service for which the customer was willing to pay. The third offer was a menu approach to pricing that enabled customers to self-select the level of service they were seeking.

The results: a reduction in discounting, higher retention, and improved profitability.

As a final comment on Level 4 strategies, we want to ensure that we have not drawn a picture of "A Bridge Too Far." Optimization is a difficult subject for B2B companies. Data is often not available, research is a new concept, and you make significant investments in your business model (account management, support, customer incentive payments and rebates) that might confuse the question even before you start. Our advice is: "Don't panic, and don't rush it." While working on Level 3, start the discussion to define a vision of Level 4. The best practice in B2B companies is to identify a "vision team" that may spend several months determining a definition of Level 4 that works in your business. During that time, you may want to try a small pilot before completing the definition. This means that rollout could be a two- to three-year project. The key is to initiate the discussion, and start collecting data.

Pricing Infrastructure

An organization cannot achieve Level 4 unless senior leadership views pricing as a strategic capability that can help the organization gain lasting competitive advantage. Otherwise, the necessary investments and the fortitude to trust models will not be there.

At Level 4, the organization will typically make one of the following investments.

People: At level 4 the pricing team needs to be augmented with specialized analytical resources (Pricing Scientists!). The company can either hire people to do this job or outsource those analytics. Our experience is that it does not need to be one or the other, but that at some point companies will find they need access to world-class resources that can provide a high level of talent and strategic insight into what can be done in the area of optimization.

Structure: As the story has unfolded, the pricing team has started with Finance in Level 2 and likely moved to Marketing in Level 3 to bring more focus on the customer. Often at Level 4, with organizational partnerships and credibility in place, the company launches an Analytics group reporting to the president, in which Pricing plays a key role. This is not to say that the Analytics group becomes an ivory tower—far from it. However, Analytics needs a voice at the table and a say in the future direction of the firm.

Results Management: The Results Management component of the Pricing Infrastructure is central to the development of Level 3. In a sense, almost everything we have talked about here ties back to becoming more sophisticated in the way the company results are being managed. The move to Level 4 is to bring sophistication and focus to the Results Management component. Usually as part of this effort, compensation is re-aligned if it has not been dealt with earlier in the journey.

Systems: Advanced systems are a key enabler of the move to Level 4. While data integrity is a concern for Level 2, data availability and integration are the key issues for Level 4. It will be impossible to optimize customer offerings if sales data resides in the transaction system but rebate data is aggregated by customer, stripped of its connection to a transaction, and dumped into the general ledger (Financial) system. Often, the team will need to make decisions to utilize data from the plan and then adjust with actual spending later. This approach is a compromise, but rebates and other customer payments are often made on the basis of the customers' "paperwork," and it will therefore be devoid of the careful planning and allocation of resources.

Pricing software has grown rapidly in terms of its breadth of usage in the past three to five years. However, the most common software vendors still price, for the most part, at price points that are affordable only for the Fortune 500. That is changing as they race to perfect their SaaS offering.

Besides price, the most common concern we hear from companies looking at implementing pricing software is that their data and processes are a long way from being ready to use in an optimization engine. Consequently, if companies go ahead, they find that implementation takes more time and money than they originally planned. The Five Level model offers some guidance here. Simply implementing software will not catapult your organization to Level 4. There is a lot of hard work required at Levels 2 and 3 to ensure that the organization can reap the benefits. The caveat is that optimization is a broad topic. We once saw an MIT professor prove that, although the airline industry is historically unprofitable and the sum of all profits over all time is a negative number, the airlines would have lost significantly *more* money had they not utilized price optimization. While what they do is not what we would call *strategic* price optimization, they do practice price optimization as a way to increase profits.

Summary

Optimization is increasingly being applied in B2B organizations. While it is not necessary for pricing managers to be statisticians, they need to understand the three core methods—conjoint analysis (survey methodology), transactional analysis, and testing—and when to use them. Level 4 is data intensive, as you are bringing data to the table that takes pricing to the next level.

The application of science needs to be grounded on the foundation of deep customer understanding achieved in Level 3, so you cannot skip that step. In fact, it is the wisdom gained in Level 3 that makes the progression to Level 4 possible.

Senior management must be strongly supportive if you are going to make this a lasting accomplishment, and not just the "flavor of the day."

Finally, the sales, marketing, and finance departments must all understand optimization and accept its value if you are to hit the pricing bull's eye.

PRICING
solutions

Level 5—
The Master

mas•ter•y/ˈmast(ə)rē/
Noun: Comprehensive knowledge or skill in a subject.

> *"The G4 Cube was almost ostentatious in its lack of ostentation . . . but it was not a success . . . Workaday professionals weren't seeking jewel-like sculpture for their desks, and mass-market consumers were not eager to spend twice what they'd pay for a plain vanilla desktop. Jobs predicted that Apple would sell 200,000 Cubes per quarter. In its first quarter, it sold half that. The next quarter, it sold fewer than thirty thousand units. Jobs later admitted that he had overdesigned and overpriced the Cube, just as he had the NeXT computer. But gradually he was learning his lesson."*[4]
>
> —Excerpted from *Steve Jobs,*
> authorized biography of Steve Jobs

Success is never final; there is always room for improvement, and we are always learning. In fact, we have one client who decided not to include Level 5 in its corporate pricing framework because it didn't want its team to be fixated on a destination.

We admire this point of view, but we still believe there is value in setting your sights on Level 5, as long as you realize it is not an end point. Companies and people do achieve mastery, and it is helpful to understand what this accomplishment looks like.

In this chapter, we will describe world-class companies and individuals who we believe are pricing masters.

The Culture at Level 5

At Level 5, we are not introducing new processes and tools; rather, everything is done just a little better, leading to improved results.

So what are some of the subtle differences between Level 4 and Level 5 companies? They are not as obvious as those that distinguish Level 2 from Level 3, and Level 3 from Level 4. But consistently performing that little bit better is like compound interest—it adds up over time!

Four characteristics separate the Masters from the rest of the pack:

- Intense commitment to value, and passion about pricing;
- Integrated business systems;
- Significant financial returns from pricing initiatives;
- Innovative approaches to addressing pricing challenges.

Let's look at some examples of each of these.

Intense commitment to value, and passion about pricing—The CEO is the "chief storyteller" of the organization, and sets its commitment to value. If you study a company that is intensely committed to creating customer value, you will also notice that it is equally passionate about capturing a commensurate return for the value created—in other words, it is passionate about pricing!

Take, for example, Starbucks Coffee Company. In 2008, Starbucks was a company in decline, and its lofty prices were considered one of the most salient reasons for that predicament. Personal financial planners even said that one of the fastest ways to become a millionaire was to cut back on your daily latte! And many people did just that. The *San Francisco Chronicle* wrote: "Americans have decided to give up their $4 lattes . . . In 2008, a better definition of 'recession' may not exist."[5]

In his 2011 book *Onward*, Starbucks CEO Howard Schultz discusses his passion to reinvigorate the customer experience, and his unwillingness to cut prices as a means to regain the luster that the company had enjoyed for so many years:

> *"So why did I feel like Starbucks was a punching bag?"* he asks. *"The '$4 latte'—that untrue catchphrase that cast Starbucks as a symbol of excess in frugal times—was hardly the consumers' enemy during this period of economic turmoil. But it sure was an easy target.*
>
> *"I refused to give into increasing external pressures and focused on anything that would keep the company moving forward, even if at times it felt like we were going the wrong way in a wind tunnel."*[6]
>
> *"Every street I walked down had 'Sale' signs displayed in windows, from Madison Avenue's high-end boutiques to Marks and Spencer's London department store. I recall seeing one sign declaring that customers could get as much as 80 percent off. There was so much pressure to every retailer and restaurant to discount prices. The unique challenge for Starbucks, however,*

was how to honor consumers' needs for lower prices and reward our core customers' loyalty without putting Starbucks on sale. Deep discounting is a slippery slope that can be impossible to climb back up. It would also play into McDonald's game, and that was not how I wanted to compete. Starbucks would compete as we always did. On quality and service."[7]

For the most part, Starbucks held to its prices—the $4 latte still exists! But the company did offer more value to its core customers in the form of a loyalty program.

As Schultz explains:

". . . we had to do something for our core customers . . . Giving them value . . . would be much less expensive than trying to win them back. The good news was that . . . we were beginning to figure out how . . . We played with some numbers and eventually came up with the idea of a $25 Gold Card that would give cardholders 10 percent off anything they bought at Starbucks . . . Our goal was to sell 25,000 cards in the first week. We surpassed that amount in the first weekend . . . Starbucks' card programs . . . were emerging as the company's winning way to deliver meaningful value."[8]

The positive results of this commitment to value and pricing are evident in that the company completely reversed the negative margin trend it had been experiencing. Furthermore, Starbucks achieved revenue growth of over 30% while others faltered during this tumultuous period. Not surprisingly, the Market recognized the strong performance with a similar rise in Starbucks' stock price. Profit margins are lagging indicators. Time will tell whether the Market will learn to appreciate mastery in pricing before the evidence is reflected in a graph like *Figure 5.1.*

Figure 5.1

Starbucks Gross Margins

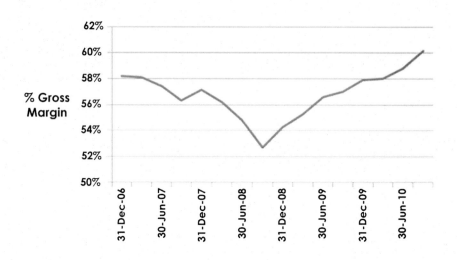

Starbucks Corporation—Analysis of Gross Margins

Integrated business systems—We have identified the importance of systems in attaining and sustaining excellence at Level 5. Pricing at this level certainly requires a holistic approach to managing and integrating a vast range of information, representing all the different perspectives that we have identified in our journey from Level 1 to Level 4—from internal systems, to market indicators, to economic factors, including:

- Costs, volumes, product families, customer groupings, and segmentations;
- Rebates, allowances, incentives, and programs;
- Competitive prices and offers;
- Transaction patterns, abandoned or lost sales;
- Customer feedback, brand health, price elasticity, promotional history;
- Social media activity, advertising, click rates;
- Commodity prices, leading indicators, consumer data.

The list above starts to suggest the endless possibilities you can use for finding variables to help you understand customer behavior and sales patterns, forecast future results, simulate expected future behavior, run scenarios, and optimize prices and returns.

Case study: Pump and Valve Manufacturer

This company had moved from Level 1 to Level 4 over the past four years. Now it was ready to progress to Level 5, but faced a significant challenge.

It had built a price structure that was based on how different customers derived value from its offering in different ways. Having the systems that enable a company to execute against this strategy is a major step that world-class companies need to master. Here is how they did it.

The company focused on linking the business drivers (in this case, rebates) to activities and events rather than financial periods. The sales team agreed to support the change if we could alleviate the work of entering and coding the rebates at period end, and provide a system for entering and approving their customer deals. The company had developed a sound price structure in Level 3, and now needed a way to update data with a live connection to the ERP and other external data. One key to building this type of connection is to avoid data that needs to be manually adjusted before it can be used in the system. In this case, we built an interface that directly accepted the customer promotion plans in a format that Sales was used to seeing and updating.

We had also found that the value of the pumps depended on the amount of capital spending in the oil fields, which was linked to a smoothed-out (200-day) average of recent crude oil prices. Pulling this data into the system was not difficult, but to use a meteorological metaphor, it moved us from simply reporting the weather to predicting it, and selecting the appropriate clothes to wear.

Over time, we tracked the deals won versus those abandoned, as well as the product mix. Tracking is interesting, but forecasting is the next logical step. We took that step, and found we could quickly improve the quality of the forecast by connecting the forecasting engine to the database and the external data. As we have said before, if you can forecast the demand curve (as complex as it is in B2B) and you know your costs, you can optimize. Running scenarios in parallel with the optimization algorithm allowed the manager to ensure his team was not treating the tool like a magic black box; business knowledge would still be necessary in the process.

The key point here is to think broadly about the problem at hand. Some kinds of information are easier to find and manage than others. Also, there are some decisions that can make your maintenance effort much easier. Finally, having the courage to move from tracking to forecasting is well worth the effort, and is the leap that puts Level 5 within your reach.

Significant financial returns from pricing initiatives— World-class companies get healthy returns from their pricing initiatives. This is what gives them the confidence to continue to make those investments. In other words, they know their payback.

An example is Marriott International. In an article titled "Marriott International Increases Revenue by Implementing a Group Pricing Optimizer,"[9] Marriott describes a new tool that it devised to help it do group pricing more effectively. This is an extremely challenging area of optimization due to the number of variables involved and the significant lead time between booking and the actual event. But world-class companies do not throw up their hands and say, "it's too difficult."

In the following quotation, Marriott demonstrates the commitment that is characteristic of world-class pricers.

> *"The aggregate actual revenue/optimal revenue . . . was 1.1 percent higher than for the same hotels*

in 2006. This equates to $46 million in revenue for 2007. As is the case with most revenue-management functions, these incremental revenues do not incur additional cost; therefore, they directly add to profit . . . The profit improvement from GPO in its first two years of use is over $120 million."[10]

Innovative approaches to addressing pricing challenges—It is not uncommon to hear Procter & Gamble referred to as an arrogant company, but it is important to make the distinction between arrogance and confidence. Our experience is that when P&G does not know something, it does not deny it and pretend it does not exist. Here is a perfect example.

The story occurs in the diaper category, in which P&G's leading competitor, Kimberley-Clarke (K-C), was making significant investments and pricing moves that P&G's Pampers team could not fully comprehend. Our experience with most companies is that, when they cannot discern their competitors' intent, they assume those competitors are "fools."

The Pampers team, however, took a different approach. They assigned one of their people to "simulate" the role of the K-C brand manager on a fulltime basis for one year. Every time the team completed a Pampers presentation, the "K-C brand manager" presented the Huggies brand plan (based on his research, competitive intelligence, and best assessment of the actions and intent of Huggies), and described how K-C would thwart Pampers' strategies. When I asked the ex-P&Ger what the Pampers team learned from this exercise, he said: "We understood [K-C's] actions much more clearly, and we gained a lot more respect for our competitor!" This kind of innovative approach to addressing a pricing challenge enables world-class companies to understand more clearly the opportunities and threats they are facing, and respond more creatively.

Who is Level 5?

One of the questions we are asked most often is "what are some examples of Level 5 companies?"

We are privileged to have many of the world's leading companies as clients, some of whom have achieved Level 5. We cannot disclose information about our clients, but there are companies that we have admired and that we believe qualify as Level 5 pricers. When we cite these companies as role models, we are not saying they are perfect by any means. To use a sports analogy, even hall of fame basketball superstar Michael Jordan missed more shots than he made (career field goal percentage was .497 on 2 pointers). Every company misses the mark sometimes, but it is the consistency of high performance and good decision-making that differentiates world-class pricers from their peers.

Earlier in this chapter we described the characteristics of Level 5 companies. Now we will go into greater depth describing two companies that have demonstrated world class capabilities.

Marriott International

Marriott has long been recognized as a highly effective pricer. The company regularly presents at leading industry conferences, and has published articles about advances it has made in pricing (revenue management).

There are many good examples of world-class capabilities in the article we mentioned earlier ("Marriott International Increases Revenue by Implementing a Group Pricing Optimizer," *Interfaces*, Volume 40, No. 1, Jan.-Feb. 2010, p. 47-57).

The following paragraphs feature some quotes that demonstrate the behaviors of a world-class pricing organization.

Pricing as a strategic priority: In 2008, at the onset of the financial crisis, many companies cut back on investments, particularly in pricing, because the prevailing wisdom was that the market would drive pricing. Marriott, however, chose a different path.

"Despite the economic downturn, Marriott International remains committed to these innovations, which reflect the wise application of operations research to challenging problems in the hospitality industry."[11]

Optimization: Marriot has been investing heavily in optimization for some time, and has achieved a superior level of competency at Level 4.

"For more than 20 years, Marriott has led the industry in the practice of Revenue Management."[12]

Integrated business systems: World-class pricing organizations have world-class data. Data richness enables them to quickly analyze and identify new pricing opportunities. These companies have limitations, like anyone else, but their limitations are completely different from those of average performers.

"Marriott is a data-rich company, and we were able to create a database containing 180 descriptions for 800,000 group requests relatively quickly. However, when we attempted to implement other steps . . . we faced several challenges for which we needed to find innovative solutions."[13]

"No competitor has anything close to the solution Consolidated Inventory / Total Yield provides."[14]

Culture change: The following quotation demonstrates that management understands that a powerful tool is not enough. Winning the minds and hearts of the sales force so that they sell value and capture the price is also extremely important.

". . . it was critical to provide high-level training to senior managers in the sales, revenue-management, and event-management disciplines to enable them to assist with change management."[15]

In J.W. Marriott, Jr.'s book *Spirit to Serve*, a chapter titled "Never Believe Your Own Hype—Or What the Press Says About You," starts by stating: "Overconfidence is such a destructive force for individuals and institutions . . ."[16]

Despite being a world-class pricer—or perhaps because of it—Marriott has not fallen prey to overconfidence.

Procter & Gamble

We have observed P&G for many years, and have admired its pricing decision-making (as we mentioned earlier in "Innovative approaches to addressing pricing challenges"). You might say we have had a front-row seat to many of the company's pricing decisions. Over the years, we have spoken to many ex-employees, read about the company, and, most importantly, worked on consulting engagements for clients who compete directly with P&G.

Here are some of the things we have observed that we believe make P&G a world-class pricing organization.

Courageous decisions: P&G demonstrates the price leadership that is required to successfully grow categories and fund innovation. Nobody likes to be first with price increases, especially with powerful retailers like Walmart, but P&G regularly steps up and leads the way.

One of the most courageous decisions it made was the move from high-low pricing to everyday low pricing (EDLP). P&G realized that high-low pricing was killing its brand value. Instead of accepting the dictates of retailers, the company made the bold move of implementing EDLP, reducing the suggested retail so that the product sold at a lower everyday price. At the same time, however, it reduced promotional spending so that the discounts were substantially less. The naysayers said the company would not succeed because retailers would punish it. But P&G held firm and other manufacturers started to follow, realizing that the high-low pricing game was unsustainable and would lead to their products being commoditized. P&G referred to this initiative as "cleaning out the swamp"—the insidious trade programs that were funding these counterproductive pricing programs. This is not to say that trade programs are no longer a problem, but only that P&G tamed the beast, thereby saving its brands from extinction at the hands of purely price-driven competition and the explosion of private-label offerings.

Use of data: P&G is a leader in the use of data to support fact-based decision-making. It was one of the first packaged-goods companies to recognize the power of pricing research and, in particular, conjoint analysis. To fully leverage the power of pricing research, the company created a position for a global pricing research leader whose responsibilities included ensuring that best practices for pricing research were being applied globally. This entailed measuring the predictive validity of past studies and maintaining a database of all studies for comparative purposes.

P&G is also highly respected for the role it plays as "Category Captain" at many different retailers. Being a Category Captain involves leveraging the retailers' POS data and combining it with other consumer research to make recommendations that will drive category growth and profitability. When these presentations are effective, they often drive better pricing decisions that benefit both the retailer and P&G.

Innovation: P&G regularly creates or reinvigorates categories. An example is the Swiffer. P&G replaced mops priced under $10 with the Swiffer system, which often cost five times more than the traditional mop. Swiffer actually made cleaning the floor fun, so that even kids wanted to use it—which greatly increased moms' willingness to pay more. While most of its competitors were trying to figure out how to build a cheaper mop, P&G was determining how to recreate the entire value proposition for a category.

You may have noticed that we have not included any B2B-focused companies. There is a reason for that. As we discussed in Level 4, B2B companies are trailing their B2C counterparts when it comes to pricing. It's not that they are slackers, or that they don't have people who are just as capable of being world-class pricers. It's that B2B business models are typically more complex. They often have thousands of SKUs and complex contracts that are negotiated with thousands of customers. They also lack the customer insight that is typically available to consumer businesses from organizations like Nielsen and others that provide rich consumer insight.

On-line-based businesses have been built thinking about Level 4 and 5 pricing concepts right from the outset. They use segmentation, transaction data, and upsell results to continually optimize (often weekly or monthly) their price and offering.

But that does not mean that B2B companies must plateau at Level 3. Indeed, we shared examples of B2B companies that have recently achieved Level 4. But very few B2B companies have attained Level 5. It is our belief, though, that B2B companies committed to world-class pricing will reach this level in the near future.

Dangers and Pitfalls

World-class companies do slip from time to time. Over the years, for example, we have admired Toyota's pricing, but the automotive manufacturer was not looking like a world-class pricer during the crisis it faced in 2010.

But first, let's look at some of the positive things we have observed about Toyota.

Share growth with less discounting: Over the years, Toyota has grown market share with less discounting than its competitors. Compared to American automakers, Toyota made far less use of promotions, did not negotiate as much, and therefore did not create a culture of discounting in which the customer walked in the door expecting to negotiate.

An example of this is the way in which the company handled the 2008 economic crisis. At a time of great uncertainty when GM and Chrysler were filing for bankruptcy, Toyota was not busy slashing prices to protect itself. Instead, it rapidly cut back on production to ensure a balance between the supply and demand of the market, and to protect pricing. I can speak of this first hand because at the time, I was in the market for a new car. Most of the car dealers were very anxious to do business, and were more than willing to discuss substantial price discounts. When I walked into the Toyota dealership, I fully expected more of the same. Instead, the salesperson provided tremendous service, staying well beyond the closing of the dealership. He was very restrained in discounting, noting: "We have a few models available, but we cut back capacity significantly so that we don't have a lot of them sitting on the lot waiting to get sold." This is a great example of a company protecting its pricing power.

But achieving Level 5 does not mean you will not face crises that will cause you to alter your pricing strategy. Toyota faced the biggest crisis of its history in 2009-2010 when it began a series of massive recalls.

As *Wikipedia* notes:

"Three separate but related recalls of automobiles by Toyota Motor Corporation occurred at the end of 2009 and start of 2010. Toyota initiated the recalls, the first two with the assistance of the U.S. National

Highway Traffic Safety Administration (NHTSA), after reports that several vehicles experienced unintended acceleration. The first recall, on November 2, 2009, was to correct a possible incursion of an incorrect or out-of-place front driver's side floor mat into the foot pedal well, which can cause pedal entrapment. The second recall, on January 21, 2010, was begun after some crashes were shown not to have been caused by floor mat incursion. This latter defect was identified as a possible mechanical sticking of the accelerator pedal causing unintended acceleration, referred to as Sticking Accelerator Pedal by Toyota. The original action was initiated by Toyota in their Defect Information Report, dated October 5, 2009, amended January 27, 2010.[1] Following the floor mat and accelerator pedal recalls, Toyota also issued a separate recall for hybrid anti-lock brake software in February 2010.[2]"[17]

The recalls struck at the heart of Toyota's value proposition—superior quality at a reasonable, but typically higher, price. They caused automotive consumers to take pause and possibly consider other alternatives, especially U.S. automotive companies that had begun to recover from 2007 and were seeking a second chance with consumers who had migrated to Toyota.

How did Toyota react? It did what it had to do to protect its market share: it discounted aggressively during this time of uncertainty. Historically, Toyota had offered fewer discounts and incentives than the competition, but at that point, it was offering more aggressive incentives.

The lesson here is that your ability to premium price is only as good as your products or services. Since that time, Toyota has suffered another disaster, not of its own making. The Japanese tsunami devastated large parts of Japan and hurt Toyota's business immeasurably. The financial results in *Figure 5.2* show the severe strain of recent events.

Figure 5.2

Toyota Financial Performance (Consolidated)*

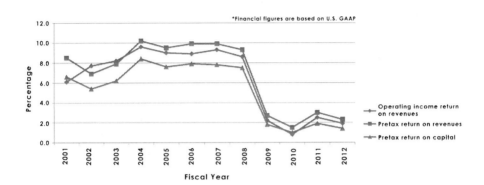

We believe that Toyota will regain its luster, but it is not something that the company can accomplish overnight. And so it is with pricing. One of the key challenges for Toyota is to ensure that it does not fall into the trap of discounting to the point that it undermines the longer-term value of the brand.

Pricing Masters

Another question on many people's minds is: "How can I become a Master?"

We thought it would be instructive to share examples of individuals we have met who we believe qualify as Masters in the pricing realm. We have had the opportunity to work with many people over the years, but there are a few who stand out. They are memorable for their commitment to pricing, their creativity, and the results they achieved.

These people all share the following characteristics:

- Passionate about pricing;
- Innovative in their approach, and able to link pricing to value very effectively;

- Very close to the customer;
- Able to protect and capture value.

Here are portraits of some of the more memorable individuals.

Neil P.

Price Mastery is needed most during times of crisis.

Neil was the president of a leading company in the electrical products industry. His middle initial was "P," which he only half-jokingly said stood for "Profit."

Neil was facing a potential crisis.

His company had invented a product that represented 40% of its revenue and 60% of its profits. The product was in essence the "Coca-Cola" of its particular category—a highly recognized and desired brand. Because of this, the company had historically charged 20% more than the nearest competitor, while maintaining dominant market share.

However, the market appeared to be changing. The sales force was getting pushback from distributors. They were saying that the price was too high and that customers were no longer willing to pay 20% more for a product that was essentially a commodity, and that there were now other good suppliers to which customers were increasingly willing to switch.

Neil's sales team was losing its confidence and increasingly saying that prices were too high.

It was a time of major uncertainty. To handle the situation, Neil knew that he had to regain confidence in the sales force. But to do that, he needed to do more than give great motivational speeches; he needed some facts.

He knew he needed some objective customer insight, and so he commissioned a pricing research study to assess the strength and longer-term viability of his company's value proposition with contractors and distributors.

The results were revealing. First, the vast majority of purchasers (i.e., electrical contractors) perceived that his company's brand was priced at the same level as the competition (it was a low-involvement purchase in which people focused on brand rather than price); they were not conscious of the price gap. Secondly, there was a small but vocal customer segment that was aware of the price gap and complained to distributors that it was excessive. Thirdly, the distributors were reacting to these complaints by telling his sales force. His sales team in turn would complain to the v.p. sales, who would then express his concerns to Neil. In essence, the noise attached to the problem intensified as it moved further up the chain of command so that by the time it reached Neil, it was like a high-school marching band!

Armed with these facts, Neil made three key decisions that would have a major impact on the company's long-term success:

- He would not cut the price of the company's core product.
- He would equip the sales team with the necessary tools, research, and training to ensure they were totally confident in their price premium and could help their distributors' customers become totally confident as well.
- He would launch a lower-priced product line under a different brand name to ensure he had a competitive offering for the price-sensitive customers.

The first step was to regain the sales team's confidence. Neil arranged for the results of the research to be presented at the national sales meeting. When the salespeople saw the research, they realized that their distributor customers had become overly sensitized to price objections by a small but vocal segment of the market, and that they had to help the distributors become more effective at handling these objections. As they left the meeting, the salespeople were given a few key slides from the research that they could share with their distributors.

The impact was immediate. The price objections from the distributors declined dramatically. The sales force in turn got its "mojo" back.

The effective handling of this potential crisis had an immeasurable impact on the company's future prosperity. This brand continues to be iconic within the electrical products industry, generating significant profits and satisfying the needs of electrical contractors.

Crisis averted. Neil rose to the challenge. He demonstrated pricing mastery.

James S.

James is another exemplary Level 5 pricer. If you were to look at an organization chart, you'd quickly see that he is actually many levels removed from the pricing function. He is one of two senior vice-presidents responsible for 11 business units representing over $15 billion in revenue.

He started a high impact pricing initiative by launching a plan to increase the focus understanding value. In one hallmark event, he brought top executives from key customers to a summit at which they were asked for open, honest, and comprehensive feedback on the performance of his companies. For two days, the facilitator guided the discussion to explore a wide variety of issues (including price) that could potentially hinder the development of customer relationships and result in sub-optimal performance. His top managers were positioned in the room in a way that clearly indicated they were meant to hear, but not interfere in, the free flow of feedback.

The event was only the launch pad for his pricing initiatives. He recognized that process and cultural (infrastructure) changes were needed as well. Not long after the launch, he kicked off a pilot project in one of the business units to bring the company's top minds to focus on one set of challenges in an effort to establish best practices and documented processes that could be agreed upon and then generalized for adoption at the other business units.

James launched a training initiative to outline the processes and tools that had been developed in the pilot, to create a vehicle for cultural change. The rollout of the training followed a very structured approach. First, the company finalized the overall pricing management process and tools based on the pilot. After developing the training materials and executing a dry run, 25 top executives representing all the business units and key staff positions came together to participate in the training, and sign off on the training package and process methodology. Then the company began to roll it out. The first classes were filled only with those who had been hand-picked to attend—those with the greatest influence on the organization.

James was also concerned about measurement. "Data driven and metric measured" was the mantra for the pricing initiative. While the slogan itself may be somewhat redundant, it was very effective at spreading the word. James set a goal that seemed impossibly high, but he made the commitment on behalf of the organization and then worked to establish a measurement framework to ensure that credible (audited) reporting was in place to track progress. His goal was a large number cumulative through five years to avoid the possibility that this would be taken as "flavor of the month." By year two, it was clear the organization was on track, and in fact, by the end of year four, it had hit the five-year target. So James, like any good executive, quickly and publicly said, "thank you; now I want you to do it again!"

Passion, change management, customer focus, and metrics—James put them all in place from a position in the organization that was well removed from the crunching of spreadsheets and building of models. But he truly is a Pricing Master.

Level 5 Strategies

Level 5 companies are able to execute more complex pricing strategies with greater alacrity than Level 4 companies. One of the most complex is Solutions Pricing. The remainder of this section is devoted to explaining the challenges and opportunities associated with this complicated, but highly rewarding, pricing strategy.

Solutions Pricing

Developing a pricing strategy for Solutions is one of the most significant challenges that our clients face. We have kept this topic out of the story until now because, while it is not the sole domain of Level 5 pricers, building an effective Solutions Pricing strategy will require many or all of the skills that you have built in your organization throughout the journey.

Let's start with a definition to ensure we are all on the same page.

Definition: *"A Solution is a combination of products and services, customized and integrated to completely solve complex customer problems".*[18]

For many companies, an ineffective definition of a Solution is their first step in the wrong direction. Without dealing with the questions of the degree of integration, and the focus on solving the problem, a Solution could become as mundane as a set of products sold on one order for a customer. A hamburger, French fries, and a cola bundles three related products to solve the problem of how to satisfy a hungry teenager, but this does not meet our definition of a Solution. In this case, the components are delivered as single entities, even though they are priced as a bundle.

The distinction between a bundle and a Solution is an important one because the prevailing pricing model for bundles is to wrap the products together, deliver them, and provide the customer with a discount for buying all the components in one order. In our definition, we include the term "completely solves" complex customer problems. To us, this means the customer is buying the performance rather than the components. Introducing a Service Level Agreement (SLA) is often the key step that moves the company from selling an integrated set of products or a bundle to selling a Solution.

Consider, for example, a global manufacturer of "smart building" equipment, such as a technology that can turn off the supply of power to your laptop charger when your laptop is in the docking station in your office, or turn off the heat or air conditioning when the office is vacant. In a large office building, the possibility of reducing power consumption when electricity rates exceed a certain threshold offers a large potential savings. If you are the facilities manager, you might consider buying all the hardware of this new technology and having a company install it in the building. In that case, you are going to be quite focused on the price of the hardware, and you may be persuaded to pay more to a supplier who has a superior value message. You hope that all these pieces will work together, but ultimately, you are responsible for making the system perform.

Now consider the alternative. Another company in the bidding changes the price structure and the value proposition. It focuses on an SLA. The company will install the hardware that it believes will best meet your needs, and the price you pay (each month) will depend on the savings the product generates. The hardware is now almost superfluous. The facilities manager has been given guaranteed economic benefits. In the Solutions offering, the facilities manager is buying the benefits rather than the hardware. It is enabled by an SLA. The hardware provider in this model now has the responsibility to update or replace aged hardware whenever the business case warrants it. If it waits too long and a component fails, the provider must pay the penalty charge in the SLA. If new technology comes out that will enable even greater savings, the provider will make the change to realize even higher fees. The ability to connect the value message, the structure of the offer, the contract, the measurement processes, the long-term relationship, the fees, and the configuration, delivery and performance of the offering in this integrated approach requires Level 5 application of the concepts we have been describing throughout the book.

The implication, then, is that to be considered a Solutions pricer, you must make the transition from selling the components to selling the benefits. Solutions pricers establish an SLA, and key the pricing to the SLA results, rather than to the cost or to the extended total of the component prices.

Some key points in establishing the offering for a Solution:

1. Solutions create extra value, and though the seller still must decide how to share the economic pie with the customer, the pie is larger.
2. Solutions are integrated, so it is hard for customers to unbundle.
3. Solutions can reduce the related expenses and risks for customers, such as:
   • dealing with multiple suppliers; and
   • integrating components and services.
4. Solutions are customized, and hence competitors will find it difficult to bid against them, or even to compare prices and features.

We have certainly met managers at businesses who find it difficult to set a price based on SLA performance rather than on the costs of the products and services they are selling. If you are going to charge a premium price for guaranteed performance, it is easy to become concerned about the other side of the coin—if performance falls short, the customer will expect you to pay a penalty. Therefore, you must clearly understand what creates value for customers, what that is worth, and your ability to deliver it consistently. As well, you will need a way to measure and report performance that is acceptable to the customer.

In *Table 5.1*, we compare the price structure of bundles versus Solutions.

Table 5.1
Bundles Versus Solutions

Component or Bundle Sale	Solutions Sale (with SLA)
• Price based on the sum of the components.	• A performance-based price structure and capture the premium.
• Likelihood of bundle discount.	• Creates the basis for a deep customer relationship.
• Risk of components becoming commoditized.	• After-sales service is the key to the offer-willing to pay penalties. Creates customer loyalty.
• After-sales parts/service is pay as you go – avoid commitment. Creates adversaries.	
• Customer takes performance risk and must purchase upgrades.	• Supplier manages performance risk using shared data, **SLA.**

Companies often face challenges when they try to move to a Solutions-based approach. There may be problems internally (such as with pricing infrastructure), as well as challenges in the go-to-market model.

For example, the global manufacturer of "smart building" equipment that could switch off laptop power and control climate had to overcome several challenges.

Not only would the SLA need to offer certainty as to the performance of this company's Solutions, but other dynamics of the marketplace would be changing as well. The sales process would be considerably different. No longer would the salespeople be selling simply to the Facilities group. Now, I/T would be involved because the Solution would need to integrate with other systems. Finance would play a bigger role because customers would want the opportunity to evaluate the alternative of purchasing the equipment as a capital item, or as a service, which is considered an operating expense. The sales team needed to be trained to sell in this complex environment. Furthermore, for someone who has been selling a product at a price, and has typically been reticent to commit to the performance of individual components, selling an SLA in which the key measurement is something broader than the performance of one piece of equipment requires a significant change in behavior.

This introduces the question of the Pricing Infrastructure changes to be considered as you move to Solutions Pricing. Think of the Results Management box in our model—and the product managers who are responsible for the P&L of their particular products. As we move into the Solutions world, the invoice will likely no longer have a line item for each component. In this case, not only is it unclear where the revenue shows up in the reporting structure, but the rest of the price waterfall costs are equally challenging to unravel. We have heard brand managers state emphatically: "We never have to give rebates on my products, so the rebates in this deal should all be allocated to the other product P&Ls." We believe that you need to tackle the issues of accountability, decision making, and reporting as soon as you establish the Solutions business. In other words, the Solutions team needs its own P&L, objectives, and time for review in the board room. If this change is the future of your business, give it a fighting chance and start managing it as a key part of the business.

In summary, Solutions Pricing is in Level 5 because it calls on all of the skills you have developed throughout this journey. Selling Solutions requires advanced application of Value-Based Pricing almost by definition, since the dimension for pricing is the SLA. There will be changes required in your go-to-market strategy, since you may face non-traditional competitors and the buying process will certainly differ. There will also be changes required for your Pricing Infrastructure as you grapple with questions of skills, structure/accountability, and measurement (as well as whether the system can create an invoice for a Solution). The upside of resolving these issues is the prospect of realizing premium prices compared to the alternative of selling a truckload of components with a bundled discount. Solutions offer the chance to align the goals of the buyer and the seller. As we have seen, when that occurs, there is a tremendous opportunity to capture value!

Summary

Mastery of any skill is not achieved easily. Just ask Malcolm Gladwell, author of several runaway best sellers such as *The Tipping Point*, *Blink*, and *Outliers*.

In *Outliers*, Gladwell claims that "greatness requires enormous time," citing The Beatles as an example. "The Beatles performed live in Hamburg, Germany, over 1,200 times from 1960 to 1964, amassing more than 10,000 hours of playing time, therefore meeting the 10,000-Hour Rule."[19]

Most executives will not spend 10,000 hours on pricing in their career. However, as you look across the business landscape of great CEOs, people like Apple's Steve Jobs, Microsoft's Bill Gates, Starbucks' Howard Schultz, and IBM's Lou Gerstner have all demonstrated mastery in pricing. Read any of their books, and you will find stories of decisions they made that made huge differences.

For example:

- How Gates wisely priced Windows in the early days of his relationship with IBM.

- How Gerstner adjusted prices of mainframes so they were positioned for the future.
- How Schultz held to his pricing and walked down the "wind tunnel."
- How Jobs learned his lessons and created PCs that had 11% market share and 35% of the category profit.

Each of these executives demonstrates the skills of pricing mastery. We believe this is because they were able to see both sides of a very important picture—value and price—at the same time, and could assess how to optimize them.

In the end, it is all about value, and all that anyone can really teach you is to make sure you know the value of your offer, and price it accordingly. If you do that, you will be successful in the long run, and will become a world-class pricer.

There is no final destination, but the journey is worthwhile!

Bibliography

1   MARN, Michael V., and Robert L. ROSIELLO. 1992. Managing Price, Gaining Profit. *Harvard Business Review* 70 (September-October):84-94.

2   RACKMAN, Neil, 1988. *Spin Selling*.

3   MARRIOTT, J.W. Jr., and Kathi Ann BROWN. 1997. *The Sprit to Serve*.

4   ISAACSON, Walter. 2011. *Steve Jobs*. Page 445.

5   SCHULTZ, Howard with GORDAN, Joanne. 2011. *Onward*. Page 159.

6   SCHULTZ, Howard with GORDAN, Joanne. 2011. *Onward*. Page 146.

7   SCHULTZ, Howard with GORDAN, Joanne. 2011. *Onward*. Page 232.

8   SCHULTZ, Howard with GORDAN, Joanne. 2011. *Onward*. Page 232.

9   HORMBY, Sharon and Morrison, Julia and DAVE, Prashant and MEYERS, Michele and TENCA, Tim. *Interfaces,* Vol.

40, No.1, January-February 2010. "Marriott International Increases Revenue by Implementing a Group Pricing Optimizer". Page 54.

10   HORMBY, Sharon and Morrison, Julia and DAVE, Prashant and MEYERS, Michele and TENCA, Tim. 2010. *Interfaces* Vol. 40, No.1, January-February 2010. "Marriott International Increases Revenue by Implementing a Group Pricing Optimizer". Page 55.

11   HORMBY, Sharon and Morrison, Julia and DAVE, Prashant and MEYERS, Michele and TENCA, Tim. 2010. *Interfaces* Vol. 40, No.1, January-February 2010. "Marriott International Increases Revenue by Implementing a Group Pricing Optimizer". Page 56.

12   HORMBY, Sharon and Morrison, Julia and DAVE, Prashant and MEYERS, Michele and TENCA, Tim. 2010. *Interfaces* Vol. 40, No.1, January-February 2010. "Marriott International Increases Revenue by Implementing a Group Pricing Optimizer". Page 48.

13   HORMBY, Sharon and Morrison, Julia and DAVE, Prashant and MEYERS, Michele and TENCA, Tim. 2010. *Interfaces* Vol. 40, No.1, January-February 2010. "Marriott International Increases Revenue by Implementing a Group Pricing Optimizer". Page 51.

14   HORMBY, Sharon and Morrison, Julia and DAVE, Prashant and MEYERS, Michele and TENCA, Tim. 2010. *Interfaces* Vol. 40, No.1, January-February 2010. "Marriott International Increases Revenue by Implementing a Group Pricing Optimizer".

15   HORMBY, Sharon and Morrison, Julia and DAVE, Prashant and MEYERS, Michele and TENCA, Tim. 2010. *Interfaces* Vol. 40, No.1, January-February 2010. "Marriott International

Increases Revenue by Implementing a Group Pricing Optimizer". Page 54.

[16] MARRIOTT, J.W. Jr., and Kathi Ann BROWN. 1997. *The Sprit to Serve*. Page 109.

[17] Wikipedia. *2009-2011 Toyota vehicle recalls*. Page 1.

[18] ROEGNER, Eric V and SEIFERT, Torsten and SWINFORD, Dennis D. *McKinsey Quarterly,* August 2001. "Putting a price on solutions". Page 1.

[19] GLADWELL, Malcolm. 2008. *Outliers*.

PRICING
solutions

Index

f denotes figure; *t* denotes table

Edwards Brothers Malloy
Thorofare, NJ USA
February 5, 2016